CU00926726

WOMEN WITH ADHD

Step by Step Workbook to Overcome Distraction and Manage Your Emotions. New Exercises and Strategies to Improve Focus and Social Confidence

LUCY WILLIAMS

First paperback edition September 2022

Book by Lucy Williams

For More Info:

lucy.williams@gmail.com

Table of Contents

PART 1
DISCOVERING

PART 3
ACTING

*"People with ADHD often have a special feel for life,
a way of seeing right into the heart of matters,
while others have to reason their way methodically."*

E. M. HALLOWELL

Overview

This guideline covers recognizing, diagnosing, and managing attention deficit hyperactivity disorder (ADHD) in women's arduous journey toward adulthood.

It aims to improve recognition and diagnosis of ADHD, ameliorate the quality of life and empower women with ADHD.

Who is it For?

Yong or adult Women, Single or in a relationship and overwhelmed Mums with ADHD and their families and carers.

Getting The Care you Deserve

You are not alone if you're a woman who has struggled to find help for your executive dysfunction or other ADHD symptoms. Your symptoms are not personal failures or character flaws. They are a product of fundamental differences in your brain's neurological wiring.

The most significant benefit of treatment is seeing your life improve. Therapy helps you accept and understand your symptoms. Explore your treatment options and get the support you need to start on the more straightforward path to a calmer mind.

PART 1
Discovering

"The real voyage of discovery consists not in seeking new landscapes, but in having new eyes."

M. PROUST

Chapter 1
What is ADHD

The attention-deficit/hyperactivity disorder (ADHD) is one of childhood's most frequent neuropsychiatric disorders, characterized by attention, hyperactivity, and impulsiveness problems. There are two different ADHD subtypes: predominantly inattentive presentation. It is complicated to organize their work, pay attention to details or follow orders; the person is easily distracted and forgets. b) Hyperactive-impulsive. The person fidgets a lot and talks nonstop; they are hyperactive and impulsive resulting in many accidents c) Combined presentation. The symptoms of the above subtypes coexist in this category (1).

This literature review aims at identifying the unique characteristics of ADHD symptoms in all stages of a woman's life, from childhood to menopause.

Awareness of these signs is essential to provide the best quality of health care for ADHD women.

To identify the unique characteristics of ADHD symptoms in all stages of a woman's life, from childhood to menopause, to provide the best health care for ADHD women. The attention-deficit/hyperactivity disorder (ADHD) is the most frequent.

Diagnosis

A specialist psychiatrist should only make a diagnosis of ADHD. A pediatrician or other qualified healthcare professional with expertise in the diagnosis of ADHD based on:

A complete clinical and psychosocial assessment of the person; should include discussion about behavior and symptoms in the different domains of the women's everyday life and:

- An entire developmental and psychiatric history
- Observer reports and assessments of the person's mental situation.

A diagnosis of ADHD should not be made only based on the rating scale. Rating scales such as the Conners' and the Strengths and Difficulties Questionnaire.

For a diagnosis of ADHD, symptoms of impulsivity/hyperactivity and inattention should:

- Meet the diagnostic criteria in DSM-5 or ICD-10[1] and

cause at least moderate social, psychological, and educational or occupational impairment based on interview and direct observation in multiple settings

- Be pervasive, occurring in 2 or more critical settings, including social, familial, educational, and occupational backgrounds.

As part of the diagnostic process, including an assessment:

- Coexisting conditions, social, familial, physical health or occupational circumstances, and educational. For young people, there should also be an assessment of their parents' or carers' mental health.

ADHD should be considered in all age groups, with all the same symptom criteria adjusted for age-appropriate changes in behavior.

In the clinical significance of impairment resulting from the symptoms of ADHD in children and young people, their views should be taken into account wherever possible.

ADHD is too often overlooked in Women. This needs to change.

Undiagnosed ADHD in women and young people has far-reaching consequences that can impact every area and step of a woman's life. While an early diagnosis is best, at any age. An ADHD diagnosis, in childhood or beyond, is the first and most crucial step toward managing all the symptoms. A fast diagnosis can change a life.

But this is not easy for many women whose ADHD is routinely missed or misdiagnosed. This is mainly because the disorder often presents differently in females and males — manifestations influenced by biology or societal standards, among other factors. The clinical criteria are not set up to account for these differences.

What Clinical Criteria Misses for Females with ADHD

It's easy to assign the ADHD label if we're talking about a young boy with a lot of energy. In the classroom, he bounces off his seat, interrupts his teacher, and distracts his classmates – the "perfect" ADHD representative. And the DSM-5 would align these signs and symptoms with an ADHD diagnosis for him.

Yet this stereotypical boy does not represent every person with ADHD or the variety of ways its symptoms present and affect.

This archetype is certainly not the way ADHD is often seen in girls.

While the research on girls and **women with ADHD** is still lacking, we do know that girls are not often hyperactive or impulsive – two of the three symptom categories for ADHD included in the DSM-5. Instead, girls are more likely to exhibit symptoms in the third category: **inattention**.

The Debunked Myth of ADHD

ADHD Myth #1: ADHD is not a real med disorder.

ADHD has been recognized as a TRUE AND REAL diagnosis by major medical and educational organizations. The APA (American Psychiatric Association) recognizes ADHD as a true medical disorder in its Diagnostic and Statistical Manual of Mental Disorders, the true mental health "bible" used by all psychologists and psychiatrists worldwide.

Attention, deficit hyperactivity disorder is biologically based. Research shows that it results from an imbalance of chemical messengers within the brain. The first symptoms are inattention, impulsiveness, and, sometimes, hyperactivity.

However, like other psychiatric conditions, ADHD lacks biological validity always. This means that experts still don't understand all the real natural causes, or the pathology, of ADHD. In most areas of medicine, the pathologies of disorders are extremely defined. Psychiatry, however, is an exception in this regard.

ADHD also lacks real diagnostic tests to confirm whether a person has this disorder. In its place, doctors use symptoms and other measures to determine ADHD's real symptomology.

Though scientists are working to find biological validity and diagnostic tests, there are other ways to feel confident in an ADHD diag. In the meantime. The real and first way is through something scientists call reliability. This refers to the ability of 2 different clinicians to evaluate the same child and independently come to the same diagnosis.

ADHD is a very reliable diagnosis. It is one of the reliable diagnoses in all of psychiatry, particularly child psycho. The reliability of ADHD drag. It is on par with the reliability of the design. Pneumonia with chest X-ray (an example of an objective diagnostic test). This is quite impressive. (DSM Field Trials)

ADHD Myth #2: ADHD is a new farce created by drug companies

ADHD is neither a modern phenomenon nor a purely American or Western one. Did not dream it up in response to pressure from the pharmaceutical industry or current academic forces and the drive to succeed in school.

Those are significant concerns and things that could potentially contribute to ADHD overdiagnosis. But ADHD is not explainable through this phenomenon.

If you go back a century year in medical literature, you'll see descriptions of children who look so much like children with ADHD. A year ago, that specific diagnosis didn't exist. Still, physicians described hyperactive, impulsive, and inattentive children, all the things we would put together to make an ADHD diagnosis today. The earliest reports date back to 1700.

In the 1800s, the physician Heinrich Hoffman wrote poems and illustrations to describe the guys he saw in practice. One example is Fidgety Phil, who he describes as, "Let me see if Philip can be a little gentleman. Let me see if he can sit for once at the table. But Fidgety Phil won't sit. He wriggles, and then I declare, swings backward, forwards, and tilts up his chair.

Here, Dr. Hoffman is describing, is a hyperactive, impulsive child — the same type of clinical presentation that today we would call ADHD. He also describes Johnny, a boy whose head is always wandering about in the clouds.

ADHD is a global phenomenon. We know this in epidemiologic studies of ADHD. Researchers go out into communities around the world, assessing many children and determining the rates of ADHD. This has been done in Africa, South America, Asia, North America, and the EU. And it shows us that ADHD is.

What's the rates of ADHD around the world are relatively consistent at between 6% and 7% of the population. If ADHD were most a Western phenomenon, we would see a very high % in North America and a part of Europe and a very low % in all other continents and countries. That's not what the real data are showing us today.

ADHD Myth #3: A.DHD is the result of unfair and bad parenting.

The cause is in brain chemistry, not the discipline. When a child with ADHD, for example, gets out of his seat in class, it's not because he has not been taught that these behaviors are wrong. It's because he cannot control his impulses.

Correspondingly parenting, which may involve punishing a child for things he can't control, can make ADHD symptoms worse. Professional interventions, such as psychotherapy, drug therapy, and behavior modification therapy, are usually required.

ADHD Myth #4: ADHD affects only men.

Ladies are just as likely to have ADHD as men, and gender makes no difference in the symptoms of the disorder. But because this myth persists, men are more likely to be diagnosed than girls.

ADHD Myth #5: A kid who plays video games for hours couldn't possibly have ADHD.

It is usual for a child with ADHD to be very distractible in one setting but highly focused in other locations.

Why is this? Because ADHD does not mean any attention. ADHD means dysregulated attention. Environments that are highly stimulating can lead to hyperfocus. In the more mundane and less compelling settings, you see the distractibility come to the surface.

ADHD Myth #6: Children with ADHD outgrow their condition.

More than 75% of individuals with ADHD in childhood continue to have it in adolescence. Up to 55% will continue to have it in adulthood.

Although it's been estimated that 7% of the adult population has ADHD, most of those people remain not diagnosed, and only one in four seek to treat.

Yet, with no help, people with ADHD are highly vulnerable to disorders, anxiety, and substance abuse. They often experience career difficulties, financial and social problems, and troubled personal relationships.

ADHD Myth #7: Young guys who take ADHD medication are more likely to abuse drugs when they become teenagers.

It's just the opposite. ADHD increases the possibility that an individual will abuse drugs or alcohol. Appropriate treatment reduces this risk.

It is undoubtedly true that children who have ADHD are more likely than their neurotypical peers to abuse drugs. However, it is not medication use. We know this through longitudinal studies comparing children with ADHD who take medicines with children with ADHD who are not. We follow them over time and see that the ones taking medication are at no increased risk of substance abuse compared to those who have ADHD and are not taking medication.

Moreover, the medications used to treat ADHD have been proven safe and effective over 55 years of use. These drugs do not help for ADHD, but they are highly effective at easing symptoms of the disorder: They are the first line of treatment for this reason.

What's driving this misconception is a very common mistake equating correlation with causation. The risk for substance use is ADHD, not medication.

ADHD Myth #8: Youngsters who are given special accommodations because of their ADHD are getting an advantage.

Children with ADHD are at a real disadvantage, and school policies seek to decrease this disadvantage as much as possible.

ADHD is a natural diagnosis. The studies tell us unequivocally that the diagnosis of ADHD confers risk for a host of adverse outcomes, including not completing high school, dropping out of college, teen pregnancies, car accidents, and a wide range of adverse effects.

The federal Individuals with Disabilities Education Act) aims to somewhat decrease these risks by requiring that public schools address the unique needs of all children with disabilities, including those with ADHD. Unique accommodations, such as extra time on tests, level the playing field so kids with ADHD can learn perfectly as their classmates.

ADHD Myth #9: Men and women who have ADHD are stupid.

Many well-known, high-achieving individuals from the past are thought to have had ADHD, including Abraham Lincoln, Benjamin Franklin, Mozart, Salvador Dali, and George Bernard Shaw.

Self-Compassion, the New ADHD Treatment

Recent research shows us that practicing self-compassion allows individuals with ADHD to manage symptoms more successfully in ways they may not imagine possible.

Whatever the challenges we find, we handle them better when we see them accurately. Whether life feels easy, complex, or anywhere in between, effective strategies depend on an undistorted picture of the details. When we are mired in reactivity, anxiety, or self-doubt, we stay in the same old ruts — in our minds and in our actions.

Attention deficit disorder (ADHD or ADD) amplifies those stressful emotions and self-doubt, yet precise solutions rely on seeing them accurately. If we underestimate the consequences of ADHD or deny that someone has it, we can't manage it fully. That clear-sightedness starts with seeing ADHD as affecting overall self-management skills, not focus or behavior specifically.ADHD intensifies those emotions and self-doubt, yet precise solutions rely on seeing them accurately. That clear-sightedness starts with seeing ADHD affecting overall self-management skills, not focus or behavior.

ADHD hinders the natural ability to meet goals in all situations, and it is not just a school disorder. ADHD may mean chronically setting stylish intentions and falling short. Musketeers and family say you should know more or work harder, but you're doing what you can. Children with ADHD frequently get mislabeled as recalcitrant or disinterested.

Similar negative feedback takes a risk, leading some individuals to mistrust their capability to handle their ADHD. Plans for managing ADHD bear sustained trouble, and problem-working chops involve resilience. To be flexible, we must identify with our strengths and also fete our defects as we learn.

Because of ADHD's negative effect on our Tone- perception, sustained adaptability may bear an ongoing practice of Tone-compassion.

Self-Compassion Builds ADHD Adaptability

The idea of Tone- compassion is straightforward. We do not mentally treat ourselves nearly as well as we'd a close friend or child. That situation has natural- life counteraccusations, potentially eroding our Tone- image, confidence, and overall happiness through the times.

Tone- compassion is a reality-grounded cure to tone- review and perfectionism. We learn to value Tone- enhancement and take responsibility for miscalculations without inner heckling. Exploration shows that Tone- compassion improves our passions, problem- working and continuity, and how we treat others. It builds adaptability when facing the goods of ADHD, too.

Perhaps you revealed a mug of coffee on the papers you brought to an important meeting. What are your first studies? You might suppose," I always squinch up, nothing ever works out, what an idiot I am.

Now try this with me. Imagine watching your nearest friend do the same introductory meetings, coffee tumbles, and ruined papers. What are your responses to your friend's boobs? It's OK, and everyone does it! Take a nanosecond, and it'll each work out. With training, we can shift that kind of compassion onto ourselves, the way we'd approach a floundering friend.

There is a misperception that a perfectionistic and critical station keeps us motivated. Exploration shows else. Perfection is insolvable to achieve. Seeking for it removes provocation, leaving us no room to fail and recover. As we'd tell anyone differently, succeeding requires the desire to alleviate and the space to stumble and move forward.

A good mindset relies on a belief that our trouble matters. How would we advise a child? You made a mistake. Now, what can we do next? This patient view leaves further room for progress, problem-working, and long-term trouble. With training, we cultivate a more balanced view of ourselves, our lives, and our ADHD.

Self-Compassion, and Substantiation - Grounded ADHD Care

How do awareness and Tone- compassion support someone with ADHD? They help us realize that Tone- image and Tone-mistrustfulness aren't hardwired internal traits but habits. Can change. A typical tone-compassion practice has three corridors observing what's going on right now(awareness), connecting with others(frequently called" common humanity"), and diligently developing and erecting a healthier tone- perspective.

Awareness means seeing life as it is. Else, we get caught up in denial, fear, wrathfulness, shut down, or lash out. Being" aware" does not mean all is OK. It also means accepting when we're unhappy — maybe admitting we're overwhelmed by our kiddies or do not know what to do. Take it all in; nothing to fix yet, but this is how the effects are for me.

Connection with other people helps make them adaptable. With or without ADHD, our struggles frequently make us feel separate and unique in our shortcomings. It seems that we're the only person who screws up or whose child fails a class or misbehaves. ADHD is common. With or without it, we all scuffle with commodities. The alternate part of Tone- compassion practice is reminding ourselves that everyone(or every parent or everyone with ADHD) has struggles. We profit from a sense of community.

The last aspect of the practice is to start treating ourselves as we'd stylish musketeers. It's not that we are perfect or do not need to fix commodities, but we can push back against the incredible voice of Tone- review. We concentrate on better intentions for ourselves" May I be strong and kind to myself now." Without seeking to make anything magical, we remind ourselves how we'd treat a friend in the same situation.

Exploration suggests that Tone- compassion practice can be profound for anyone. With ADHD, rehearsing Tone- compassion builds a foundation for positive changes while navigating whatever additional ADHD care requires. Tone- understanding will enable individuals to flourish in ways they may not have believed possible. And that's precisely the point of the practice.

DIY Self-Compassion for ADHD Minds

Can use the following exercise in two ways. As with all awareness, the broader intention is to make traits through reiteration. We exercise so that a new way of thinking is ingrained. One approach is to set a timekeeper for several twinkles (anywhere from five to 15 flashes will do) and follow these instructions by sitting or lying down comfortably. However, aim to remain alert and upright, If sitting. Either close your eyes or shift your aspect to commodity-distracting.

Take many deep breaths. Gather your attention, which may catch up in Tone- imputation, fear, joy, worries, or anything different. For now, concentrate on the movement of your body with each full breath.

Next, with each inhalation, observe it all. You might say." This is what my experience is now. Or "That is how it feels, for better or worse." Also, consider," Everyone has moments like this one."

With every exhalation, set an intention" May I find strength and kindness for myself right now." Use any expression that feels natural, commodity you would say to comfort a friend.

You'll get distracted nearly incontinently. That is what our mind does. Treat that distraction the same way it happens; no need for frustration. Come back to take the coming breath.

Continue this way for many breaths or until your timekeeper goes off.

Alternately, at any moment, you can reset your perspective. For many breaths, remind yourself," Right now, amid this stress, may I remain solid, predicated, and kind to myself. "That becomes easier over time, especially when combined with frequent contemplation practice.

Chapter 2
Gender Difference in ADHD

" Too bad for them if they fall piecemeal upon discovering that women are not men or that the mama does not have one. But is not this fear accessible to them? Wouldn't the worst be, is not the worst, that women are not devitalized, that they've only to stop harkening to the Enchantresses(for the Enchantresses were men) for history to change its meaning? You only have to look Medusa straight on to see her. And she's not deadly. She's beautiful, and she's laughing"
HELENE CIXOUS

We Are Not the Same

Both men and women can have attention deficiency hyperactivity complaints (ADHD). But only one woman is diagnosed with ADHD for every two men diagnosed. Why? ADHD exploration has concentrated on males and hyperactive, impulsive symptoms. ADHD in women frequently presents with different symptoms than it does in men. These symptoms do not match ADHD conceptions and are commonly confused for other conditions.

It's important to note that ADHD can affect a person no matter where they fall on the gender diapason. Given the current exploration of ADHD in women, this composition refers to gender in the double sense. Read on to learn further about ADHD in women.

Substantiation suggests that the frequency of ADHD is more significant in males than in ladies. Likewise, ADHD is more generally diagnosed in adult males than in adult ladies. There are a lot of differences for the genders in the incarnation of ADHD symptoms in nonage.

Parents and preceptors are generally ignorant that symptoms in girls differ from those in boys. ADHD girls aren't ordinarily hyperactive. On the negative, they tend to have increased attention deficiency as part of the complaint. Girls are also more likely to suffer from low Tone- regard, underachievement, and anxiety and depression diseases than boys and are more likely to start smoking or get pregnant while still in the middle or high academy. But boys suffer from hyperactivity, advanced impulsivity, and tardy actions, while the complaint seems to prevail greatly.

Chapter 3
Women with ADHD

No More Suffering in Silence

Exploration shows that ADHD exacts a tremendous risk on women than it does on men. Clinicians need different tools for diagnosing and treating the complaint across genders, and women learn better how the condition affects them.

Utmost mainstream exploration of attention deficiency complaint (ADHD or ADD) shows no significant differences in how the condition presents in men versus women. That is, on utmost measures, data suggests that the relations witness the same type, number, and inflexibility of symptoms, the same academic struggles, the same number of comorbid diseases, and the same efficacity of the drug.

But the lived gests of real women make it clear that this is not the whole story. Women with ADHD face numerous of the same symptoms as their male counterparts. Still, they also labor under the added burden of restrictive gender places, shifting hormones, and a lesser tendency towards Tone- mistrustfulness and Tone- detriment. And arising exploration reveals that while their diurnal symptoms may image each other, men and women with ADHD face dramatically different issues in the long term.

Sometimes, the ADHD establishment and women themselves accept that gender differences play a more significant part in life with attention deficiency than preliminarily allowed. Then is how we can start to make sense of the womanish ADHD experience.

How Can Our Model Include Women?

ADHD was first defined and grounded on the actions of hyperactive boys. Indeed, until 2012, ADHD was grouped with the Disruptive Behavior diseases of Childhood in the Diagnostic and Statistical Manual(DSM I- IV). The presumption remains that the individual criteria for ADHD pertain as directly to inattentive women than to hyperactive boys. Quantitative assessments still concentrate on external actions that intrude on other people. Still, utmost women struggle with an internalized impairment that affects their sense of Tone and qualitative life operation chops. To accommodate the newest data on women's guests, the abstract ADHD model has to shift down from geste and toward impairment.

The differences in donation and impact reflect a gap in our evolving understanding of women and ADHD. Due to their inattentive symptoms and tend to internalize their passions, women's modest donations can fluently be misinterpreted. A woman's despairing about untreated laundry or being late to her child's recital might be dismissed as anxiety or a mood complaint. Still, the customary underpinning passions of inadequacy and Shame are delicate to admit and articulate and further grueling for clinicians to fete or quantify. Seeking to hide their differences and reticent to ask for help, women second guess themselves and retreat when their credibility is questioned.

What Is the Power of Gender places?

Numerous women feel that conforming to gender part prospects is the route to acceptance. Societal demands for communication and cooperation bear the perfect choreography of administrative functions. Still, women with ADHD are baffled by changeable administrative functions. Overwhelmed and frantic, they accept that they aren't entitled to a support system but that they're the support system.

Why Do Women with ADHD Have a Bad Sense of Tone?

Women with ADHD condemn themselves for being too distracted to" catch up" with daily liabilities. They allow their lack of provocation, disorganization, or belatedness to define them and anticipate review or rejection. Ashamed of their emotional reactivity, numerous bowdlerize rather than unhappy threat responses. Nevertheless, when lower guarded at home, their frustration triggers outbursts directed at mates or children. Similar unintended occurrences leave them feeling demoralized and overwhelmed with remorse. Without a neurobiological explanation, they attribute these crunches to a flawed character.

Signs and Symptoms of ADHD in Women

numerous women with ADHD live with a painful secret" Shame, unfortunately, seems to be the name of the game for innumerable women I've worked with who have ADHD," said Terry Matlen, MSW, ACSW, a psychotherapist and ADHD trainer.

She said that women with advanced degrees in demanding, high-powered positions feel overwhelmed once they get home, stressed out by all ménage details." They feel like they're living a taradiddle — that their accomplishments are simply due to good luck."

Indeed for women who understand how ADHD makes daily life delicate, one minor mistake or overlooked task can shoot them reeling from demotion " like simply forgetting to subscribe their child's academy-related paper in time."

This triggers a shower of negative, cruel studies" Oh no! I have done it again. What's wrong with me? I am such an idiot!"

In nonage, girls are tutored that we must keep a tidy home, cook regale all night, entertain, take care of the chores, raise well-conducted children and work full time.

For women with ADHD, these unrealistic and illegal prospects can amplify their Shame and weaken their Tone- regard. She said this happens substantially when women become parents because of numerous fresh liabilities.

When they can not keep up, they start feeling shamefaced. They rebuke themselves for not being what they perceive as good enough maters. They worry their kiddies will not learn specific chops like time operations. She said they regularly compare themselves to other mothers, for whom parenthood and different fatherhood-related liabilities feel to come snappily.

"Women are tutored to be a stabilizing force in the family. However, also what? So she continues to live with her terrible secrets of feeling shy, unintelligent, If she falls piecemeal."

Numerous women with ADHD also have been told that ADHD is not an" actual" condition, said Matlen, who also has ADHD. They are told they need to work harder, but" Telling a woman to try harder is like asking someone with a hail impairment to hear better."

Letting go of Shame and passions of inadequacy is a process that takes time. Seven Tips.

ADHD Symptoms as Endured by Girls

We know there is so much further to ADHD than these broad orders, especially when we are considering how it presents in girls. A commodity as simple as picking cuticles can be a subtle sign of ADHD!

Also, there is the little girl who'll talk your observance off and always has her head in the shadows, featuring the day down. And the girl who noway seems to pay attention in class but always goes over and further on every assignment and gets fantastic grades.

The signs are also there in the youthful woman who seems to have everything figured out — until she reaches council. In over her head, she's persistently anxious, held back by her fear of failure and scrabbling to put the pieces of her life come back together.

These signs of ADHD are frequently missed in ladies. At worst, these signs may be misinterpreted as shiftlessness, irresponsibility, rudeness, or another negative quality. Parents, for illustration, may scold their son for forgetting to do schoolwork or having a messy bedroom, viewing both as clear signs of irresponsibility — somewhat symptoms of ADHD.

How to Increase the Possibility of Getting the Good opinion

When you go to a hospital for an evaluation, describe the applicable substantiation-grounded issues and ask that they consider the possibility of underpinning ADHD

* Inattentive symptoms
* Internalizing symptoms
* Emotional dysregulation
* Late adolescent onset
* Low Tone- regard
* Eating dysregulation

- Habitual anxiety
- Habitual relationship problems
- Perfectionistic geste
- Substance dependence
- Sensitive hypersensitivities
- Habitual restlessness
- Disinclination to read
- Occurrences of rage or gashes
- Frequent perversity
- Picking actions
- Violent premenstrual symptoms

What Are Implicit Issues for Undiagnosed Women?

As women's liabilities increase, their cerebral torture increases, but low Tone- regard infrequently allows their requirements to come first. Detracted from their Tone- care, women with ADHD defer checks and procedures and function with severe sleep poverties. Inconsistent eating patterns, shaped by impulsivity, can affect complications. Chronically stressed, they may depend on traditional specifics to manage anxiety, mood diseases, sleep, or pain or Tone- rehabilitate with alcohol or medicines.

As women develop, they become less characteristic, yet their suffering continues as their healthy-guarded secret. They may part themselves from musketeers and hide their despair from mates. Believing in their unworthiness, they may endure connections involving emotional and physical abuse. Similar forlornness, combined with impulsivity, contributes significantly further to Tone- detriment than men. Indeed more concerning is their necessary lesser liability for suicidal studies and attempts. Recent studies suggest that girls with ADHD quickly die earlier of unnatural causes, primarily due to accidents.

These starkly elevated threat factors rate attention as a public health extremity. But these issues are avoidable. Healing begins with a safe connection to a person who becomes a lifeline to acceptance and support.

ADHD in Adolescent Ladies

There's strong substantiation that ADHD children have problematic psychosocial development and maladjusted nonage. The signs furnishing such a condition comprise unacceptable academic achievement, difficulty in interpersonal connections with the family and peers, injuries, and comorbidity with other psychiatric diseases. The development of the brain, about the anterior lobe relating to administrative function chops, similar to working problems, working conflicts, and controlling impulses, occurs in nonage and continues up to the age of 25. still, in ADHD people, the development of this brain region is delayed, and as a result, the lack of the below chops induces anxiety and aggressive or dysfunctioning geste. Inattention, the typical characteristic in ADHD girls, is linked to more minor disorganizing symptoms compared to the bones of the hyperactive subtype characterizing boys. As a result, adolescent girls remain undiagnosed in their inviting maturity.

Likewise, this period includes fresh challenges for the girls, similar to low Tone- regard, social pressures, prospects of maturity by parents and preceptors, and sexual enterprises. Studies have shown that due to low Tone- regard, adolescent girls with ADHD are frequently driven to seek confirmation via the sexual attention of others. Thus, ADHD girls run two times further in gestation than their peers without ADHD.

ADHD During the Reproductive Period

This is an adding belief that the possibility of ADHD girls still having the complaint in the majority is decisive. The mean age of ADHD in women who haven't been diagnosed in nonage is 36 to 38 times

because of comorbidity or their children being diagnosed with ADHD.. Before that, they're generally incorrectly diagnosed with mood or anxiety complaints. Indeed if they're secondary conditions, their treatment doesn't reach the root of the problem, ADHD. Studies show that the first two weeks of the menstrual cycle are smoother for ADHD women than the other two when the progesterone situations increase. During the third and fourth week, called the luteal phase, progesterone decreases the salutary goods of estrogens on the brain, conceivably dwindling the drug's effectiveness as well. There's the belief that ADHD women present more severe premenstrual symptoms than women without ADHD It seems that per zilches contraceptives alleviate ADHD symptoms in numerous women, minimizing hormonal oscillations. Three weeks of taking estrogen contraceptives followed by a week with progesterone only feel especially useful in dwindling the symptoms.

ADHD During The Perinatal Period

There aren't numerous studies assessing ADHD progression in gestation, but the hormonal changes of this period feel to have some impact on the complaint course.

Gestation and parturition produce a sense of disequilibrium in utmost matters. Although essential ADHD symptoms in gestation drop due to estrogen increases, women have different attention distraction symptoms as they concentrate on motherliness and their new part. In the postnatal period, estrogen situations radically drop, dwindling dopamine situations and performing in a depressive mood. The typical characteristics of ADHD in pregnant women are comorbid psychiatric diseases and low tone- regard, while maters with clinical or sub-clinical ADHD symptoms feel more vulnerable. In recent exploration related to ADHD results in gestation and labor, women diagnosed with ADHD at any stage of pregnancy had 20-30 further chances of having a cesarean section; also, their babies had an inversely increased chance of support to start breathing or to be taken into a neonatal unit. Other Centers for Disease Control studies on the impacts of pharmacotherapy in gestation showed that numerous pregnant women take the drug for ADHD. Women who took the ADHD tablet in the first trimester of pregnancy had a further possibility of giving birth to a baby with inheritable anomalies (gastroschisis, omphalocele, transverse branch insufficiency) than women who hadn't taken ADHD drugs. Limited data also live for the use of medicines by maters during breastfeeding. As instigations at the end of gestation can negatively affect fetus development, the exposure of babies via motherly milk could affect the outgrowth of babies and hurt their appetite and sleep. Postpartum women with

ADHD can present deterioration of symptoms after labor with the donation of depressive symptoms. The new challenges of maters in the postnatal period affect functional chops, chops that ADHD women were formerly trying to achieve throughout their lives. However, ADHD symptoms can come back, If they've chosen to stop their specifics. ADHD symptoms are analogous to those of depression, and the symptoms of anxiety are shadowed by the bones of ADHD. numerous women in the postpartum period

are diagnosed with depression because clinicians may not know the particular characteristics of ADHD in women and may concentrate on comorbid diseases. Unfortunately, numerous women with ADHD admit treatment for other conditions but not for

ADHD. Semple et al. proposed in 2011 to check women in the perinatal period for depression and ADHD symptoms.

ADHD in The Menopause Period

As shown above, during her life, a woman can experience various regular hormonal changes starting from preadolescence up to menopause. During perimenopause and menopause, estrogen and progesterone levels decline, and ADHD becomes more severe. Perimenopause in the story leading up to menopause. It could take a few months or ten years, though the average time is four years. During this period, estrogen levels decline, and ovaries stop releasing eggs. Menopause occurs immediately after this phase. The decline of estrogens that until then affected the release of neurotransmitters serotonin and dopamine induces various changes in the brain's biochemistry. Dopamine deficiency is responsible for presenting ADHD symptoms, whereas serotonin deficiency leads to depressive mood. Given thus that dopamine is the trademark of ADHD, this additional change can lead to even more difficulties with focusing and concentration. As postmenopausal women run a higher risk of osteoporosis and cardiovascular conditions, they also have to face the potentially changing psychiatric disorders that can make the solution to the problem more difficult; whereas it is considered more possible for postmenopausal women also who have ADHD to be more vulnerable to the mood disorders of menopause

There's no available exploration on menopause and ADHD, but the abundance of anecdotal substantiation supports a link between the two. Numerous of my cases with ADHD report that existing symptoms worsen in menopause. Some patients also report new onset of symptoms, though I find numerous cases were" frame" or" mildly" ADD throughout their life.

likewise, exploration has not yet established how frequently ADHD is diagnosed for the first time during menopause – a vital hand to consider, given that menopause and ADHD in after majority share numerous symptoms and impairments, including but not limited to

* Mood lability
* Poor attention attention
* Sleep disturbances
* Depression

These parallels indicate an imbrication in the clinical donation and conceivably underpinning brain mechanisms.

Still, the closest we have come to examine this relationship has been a series of studies on women WITHOUT ADHD. They were treated with ADHD drugs for onset cognitive problems and ADHD- suchlike symptoms related to menopause. The studies show that atomoxetine and Vyvanse ameliorate administrative functioning in healthy menopausal women, and that the ultimate activates organizational brain networks as revealed by neuroimaging. These findings suggest that some women may profit from ADHD drugs to treat cognitive impairments during menopause.

Menopause and ADHD Implicit Treatments and Interventions

Menopause is a period of life in which the woman is in the throes of a cognitive and hormonal upheaval which then falls on an emotional alteration. However, these characteristics are also typical of ADHD. Therefore, they share a unique and complicated relationship. Although evidence-based medicine based on anecdotal data confirms this time and time, data-based science on randomized clinical trials is still very scarce. The reason is a poor representation of the female gender in medical sciences and for women with ADHD.

In this section, we will learn more about the role of so-called female hormones such as estrogen, how hormonal fluctuations and menopause can affect neurotypical women, and how this can help inform clinical approaches for women with ADHD.

During perimenopause and menopause, numerous women witness cognitive changes that mimic and can be confused with attention deficit hyperactivity disorder (ADHD or ADD). Let's try to understand together how the hormonal changes typical of menopause affect women who have ADHD. Wisdom, unfortunately, is not there. Despite the growing and monstrously justified interest, no studies specifically look at menopause in women with ADHD. This severe clinical gap needs to be addressed in the future.

Despite this, however, we can take advantage of the medical knowledge on menopause in general as well as on hormonal fluctuations and the role of estrogen in this period and try to put the pieces together and understand how they affect what we can define "ADHD-like" symptoms, and as doctors, therapists and caregivers can set up treatment for this group of women.

Pharmacological Interventions

These treatments and interventions target neurotransmitters that are affected by the loss of estrogen and may help women with ADHD during menopause. In confluence with psychiatrists, gynecologists(with grit in the hormonal operation of menopause) may form similar cases of care brigades.

Estrogen relief, a form of hormone remedy(HT), is a standard treatment to help palliate or lessen symptoms of menopause. Cases should consult with their clinician regarding this intervention. Recent exploration shows that the combined estrogen-progesterone form of HRT may increase the threat of bone cancer. Still, the danger is reasonably low. 15 Studies on estrogen-only HRT are inconclusive, with some indicating no or indeed reduced threat for bone cancer, while others show some(standard) bone cancer threat. Overall, recent exploration suggests that the danger of using any type of HRT is lower than preliminarily reported in the literature. As far as other benefits, studies show that HRT, if initiated within ten times of menopause, reduces each-beget mortality and pitfalls of coronary complaint, osteoporosis, and madness.

Instigations, which increase dopamine's vacuity, is known to alleviate ADHD symptoms and administrative functioning.

Adding a low cure of estrogen may help compound goad good. Transdermal forms of estrogen may be stylish to minimize systemic side goods (may acclimate goad tablets with the addition of estrogen.)

Picky serotonin reuptake impediments (SSRIs) may help regulate mood/ depression and reduce anxiety symptoms.

S-adenosylmethionine (SAMe) has been shown to have antidepressant parcels and may be a promising volition to SSRIs for those that find them delicate to tolerate.

Acetylcholinesterase impediments, like Aricept, are approved to treat cognitive poverties associated with Alzheimer's. Off-market, they've been used to treat ADHD with varying results.19- you may use this class of medicines with instigations or estrogen to help menopausal women with ADHD.

Non-Pharmacological Interventions

Psychotherapy Cognitive behavioral remedy(CBT) may help make and support administrative function and other cognitive chops(time operation, planning, etc.) affected by menopause. Dialectical geste remedy may help with emotional regulation.

Understanding the menopausal transition and the symptoms may lessen patient response.

Awareness-grounded practices may ease menopause symptoms.

life changes and healthy habits(exercise, sleep, stress reduction, etc.) may likewise offset symptoms of menopause.

While there's interest in the efficacity of phytoestrogens, sauces, and other supplements, exploration has not established with these natural approaches effectively treat menopause symptoms. Cases who prefer this route should consult with naturopathic croakers.

Menopause and ADHD Conclusions

Estrogen loss during all the stages of menopause affects several important neurotransmitters that regulate cognitive function and emotion, causing some women to witness physical and internal changes ranging from mild to severe. We don't know how to predict who'll detect these impairments or why. Also, menopause symptoms unequivocally mimic ADHD symptoms and may be one medium for" adult-onset ADHD."

Research has not determined whether women with ADHD are more affected by menopause. But given what we know about ADHD and the impact of estrogen loss on executive functioning in non-ADHD women, we can assume that women with ADHD are more vulnerable to difficulties during menopause. Treatments for menopausal women with ADHD should consider the colorful considerations we've bandied then.

How Do Comorbid Conditions Complicate the Picture?

Most women with ADHD generally struggle with more than one comorbid problem, and those symptoms are frequently the most observable. Accordingly, women are commonly misdiagnosed and treated for anxiety and mood diseases as primary judgments. Their physiological expressions of anxiety manifest in fleshly complaints ranging from headaches and nausea to nail-smelling or cuticle-selecting. They're more likely to present with dysregulated eating patterns and an advanced BMI. They're more likely to have personality diseases, with Borderline Personality complaints being the most common. They show substance abuse or compulsive shopping, or gambling. They may describe sensitive load, acuity to touch, sound, light, or smells. They're more likely to have endured early physical or sexual abuse and may manifest symptoms related to PTSD. All combination of these comorbid issues creates a difficult individual picture.

Take-Home dispatches for Women with ADHD

exploration must explore why ADHD exacts a far lesser risk on women. Maybe the perfect storm of internalized symptoms, hormonal oscillations, and the pressure of societal prospects combine to produce an environment of stressors unique to ladies. Attributing their difficulties to their character failures feeds the Shame and dismay that can undermine them. Because girls with ADHD are more reactive than visionary, they gradationally lose confidence in their judgment since it frequently betrays them.

Compared to boys, women with ADHD perceive themselves as further disabled and their experience of adverse events as further painful. They're more likely to condemn themselves for their difficulties and feel lucky if the effects turn out well. They're more likely to struggle with low Tone- regard and Shame. It shows that women with ADHD are more vulnerable to their perceived failures in Tone- regulation than men. But what if the experience of men isn't considered the standard?

These differences suggest that studies comparing girls with ADHD to girls without ADHD would yield lesser particularity about the impact of ADHD.

We can not direct the wind, but we can acclimate our cruises. Women with ADHD can not change their brain wiring but can reframe their guests through a different lens. They can learn to embrace their unique aptitudes, celebrate the creativity of non-linear thinking, establish new precedences grounded on Tone- acceptance, and find ADHD-friendly surroundings where they can thrive. Immaculately, an ADHD opinion is the first step toward reversing their destructive belief system. It offers a neurological explanation for why effects are so hard and offers confirmation that allows them to enjoy their successes.

Chapter 4
Sex, Hormones, and Brains

"Couples who schedule a time to connect have healthier,
happier relationships."
CHRIS KRAFT, PH.D.

I t has been proven that hormones affect the nervous system and the neural circuits in the fetal period. While men have further considerable brain volume than women, there are veritably significant differences between the two genders. Men have a bigger amygdala and hypothalamus, while women have larger hippocampus. Estrogen receptors are located in the hypothalamus, while androgen receptors are in the amygdala. Hormone oscillations during transitional ages in a woman's life affect brain functions, similar to the brain's armature, metabolism, and hematosis. For illustration, some suggest that estrogens in postmenopausal women increase supplemental cerebral blood inflow. thus, it's necessary to consider the part of coitus hormones in brain function. The natural hormonal changes in the menstrual cycle phase, postpartum period, perimenopause, and menopause, and external hormonal use, similar to combined oral contraception and hormonal remedy at menopause, constitute critical variables and are significant to be taken into account.

How Do Hormones Connect to ADHD Symptoms?

Beginning at puberty, yearly hormonal oscillations bring high situations of estrogen and progesterone, enhancing neurotransmitters and perfecting cognitive functioning following the period. Still, women witness worsening ADHD symptoms and typical premenstrual changes when premenstrual hormone situations drop. Low estrogen triggers more significant perversity, mood, sleep, and attention dislocations. These observable symptoms can fluently lead to a PMDD opinion without considering underpinning ADHD.

As estrogen situations drop throughout menopause, **ADHD symptoms** consolidate. Combined with age-related cognitive changes, confusion, memory, attention, and sleep become more disabled. Since girls now spend about a third of their lives post-menopause, experimenters must explore the impact of hormonal cycles on ADHD symptoms.

Hormonal Fluctuations by the Lifespan Estrogen

To understand menopause's symptoms, you must first understand **estrogen** and how its oscillations impact women.

Estrogen is the hormone responsible for girls' and women's sexual and reproductive development. Estrogen also modulates the functioning of numerous psychologically essential neurotransmitters, including

* Dopamine, which plays a central part in ADHD and **superintendent performing**
* Acetylcholine, which is intertwined with memory
* Serotonin, which regulates mood

Advanced situations of estrogen are linked to enhanced super-intendent function and attention. Low or shifting estrogen situations are associated with colorful cognitive poverties and neuropsychiatric diseases like Alzheimer's and depression.

conditions of estrogen and other hormones change vastly across the lifetime and impact the mind and body in multitudinous ways. The complexity of hormonal oscillations complicates the exploration of how hormones affect cognition — particularly in **women with ADHD**.

Premenopause Menstruation and the Reproductive Times

Estrogen attention is excellent and steady during reproductive times. In the yearly menstrual cycle, estrogen situations steadily rise during the follicular phase(generally from day six to 14) and drop rashly in ovulation(around day 14). In the ultimate half of the luteal stage(the last two weeks of the cycle), estrogen situations continue to drop as progesterone increases. However, estrogen and progesterone situations fall, and the thickened uterine wall shanties during monthlies, If gestation doesn't do. Girls report emotional changes and cognitive problems at colorful cycles, especially when estrogen situations are at their smallest.

These hormonal oscillations in the menstrual cycle impact **ADHD symptoms**. As estrogen situations increase, ADHD symptoms are at their smallest in the follicular phase. Though it hasn't been studied, we can logically infer that **ADHD specifics** may be more effective at this point in the cycle. Indeed, in some studies, neurotypical ladies report more significant goad goods during the follicular phase than during the luteal phase.

The luteal phase is when you see a premenstrual pattern(PMS), a collection of physical, emotional, and behavioral symptoms brought on by dwindling estrogen and adding progesterone. Interestingly, premenstrual dysphoric complaint(**PMDD**), a severe interpretation of PMS, is more current in women with ADHD than in women without ADHD.

The Pivotal Period

The climactic times, the transition from the reproductive times through menopause, is characterized by enormous hormonal oscillations as overall estrogen situations gradually drop. These oscillations contribute to physical and cognitive changes.

What Is Perimenopause?

Before menopause is the perimenopause stage when ages come irregular – in duration(short vs. long intervals) and inflow(heavy vs. light) – but haven't yet stopped. The period for the onset of perimenopause is 47, and it can last four to ten

During this stage, total estrogen and progesterone situations begin to drop desultorily. Species of follicle-stimulating hormone(FSH) stimulate the ovaries to produce estrogen, and luteinizing hormone(LH), which triggers ovulation, also vary. FSH and LH situations initially increase as estrogen situations drop(smaller follicles remain to be stimulated), ultimately dwindling mainly and remaining at low conditions in postmenopause. OB/ GYNs frequently measure FSH and LH situations to determine if a case is in menopause.

These shifting estrogen situations help explain the occasionally extreme mood and cognitive problems that numerous ladies, ADHD or not, experience in the menopause phase.

What's Menopause?

During this period, menstrual cycles stop due to declining situations of estrogen and progesterone. The onset of menopause is 11 months after the last period, which signals the end of a woman's reproductive times. The stage following menopause appertains to postmenopause. The median age for menopause is 51.

Much research has failed to establish scientific differences between perimenopause, menopause, and postmenopause, so we're forced to consider all three of these phases under the marquee of menopause.

How Changing Hormones complicate ADHD Symptoms

One little-given side effect of meno and perimenopause? They could make your ADHD symptoms harder to manage. Then is how one businesswoman dealt with shifting hormones and stayed on top of her workload.

ADHD symptoms change as we progress and life circumstances become more complicated and stressful. Hormones, in particular, frequently complicate ADHD symptoms as women edge near **menopause**. As you've refocused out in your question, this worsening of symptoms may do during perimenopause, when estrogen situations begin to drop.

We know that when estrogen situations drop, cognition suffers. Women struggle with memory, word reclamation, and other cognitive conditioning. In fact, for some people, the change in cognitive function is so drastic that some suppose they're developing madness or Alzheimer's. Lower situations of estrogen may beget mood diseases. During this time of hormonal oscillations, we find that **ADHD** drugs and strategies for managing ADHD symptoms don't work as effectively as they formerly did.

Your new difficulty in dealing with phone calls and feeling overwhelmed when faced with multiple systems may be due to your estrogen poverties. Changing hormone situations, combined with ADHD, create a grueling problem for numerous women in the plant.

Menopause Symptoms in the ADHD

Declining estrogen situations are associated with colorful changes across all menopause stages. These symptoms can worsen and alleviate over time, though utmost physical symptoms stop after many times.

Physical Symptoms

*   Hot flashes
*   Sleep problems
*   Weight gain
*   Mood lability
*   Anxiety
*   Loss of libido

Cognitive Symptoms

*   Disabled attention and attention
*   Bloodied **working memory**

- Disabled verbal ignorance
- Overall disabled superintendents performing

Not all women will witness all these symptoms, and the impact of estrogen loss during menopause ranges extensively. The factors fueling these individual differences aren't well understood.

Chapter 5
Impact on Day-to-Day Life

Numerous girls who intentionally struggle with this complaint internalize these misconstructions. As the examens accumulate, their tone- regard plummets. They begin to feel confusion and shame and question their capability to handle putatively simple aspects of life.

A Hedge to Independent Success in Education and Career

Girls and women with ADHD frequently struggle to concentrate in the academy and the plant. While they are not dismembering others, their difficulties with focus can keep them from getting effects done. They'll frequently struggle quietly with these issues as they fall before.

Undiagnosed, some may overcompensate for the difficulties, going over and further with lists upon lists, noise-canceling headphones, and other precisely planned strategies. But it's not always enough. A Detriment to connections

ADHD can also make navigating social situations delicate. Individualities may not know why they frequently lose track of what is being said or constantly intrude during exchanges, inadvertently annoying and disturbing numerous along the way. Also, there is ADHD's a substantial impact on romantic connections.

The female with ADHD wants to be a better friend, family, son, mama, and woman, but she can not help how an undiagnosed complaint affects her socially.

A Common Beget of fresh Mental Health Issues

Low tone- regard and habitual shame frequently lead to other internal health issues and dislocations in the lives of undiagnosed women with ADHD. This helps explain why anxiety, mood diseases, and tone-harming actions are so common in this group. By the time an opinion is made, the case has probably had apparent symptoms of one of these comorbid conditions for times.

The Right Tools, Change a Woman's Life

Undiagnosed ADHD in ladies has far-reaching consequences that can impact every area of life. While an early opinion is stylish, an idea at any age can start a woman on a new path, unleashing the tools, supports, and treatments that can help her manage ADHD and ease her life.

What Needs Women with ADHD

We need to start feting ADHD in women. This is NOT a manly-specific complaint.

Women, take your enterprises seriously. Your struggles may point to ADHD if the notion seems far- brought to you. Talk to a professional and get tested. It's so essential.

Clinicians play a part, too. I have diagnosed numerous women who have been floundering with undiagnosed ADHD for times but did not meet the clinical criteria for the complaint as outlined by the DSM- 5. It's on us, as interpreters, to suppose outside these deficient guidelines to help further girls and women get the opinion they need.

Let's push for further exploration. Let's expand the symptoms of the DSM- 5 to more fit ladies. Let's get girls and women the tools they need to manage ADHD and facilitate their lives.

Other ADHD Challenges

obliviousness, disorganization, poor time operation, and comber coaster feelings were mentioned constantly by the grown-ups with ADHD who took the check. The feeling that the non-ADHD mate doesn't understand ADHD was a top complaint." My hubby chalks up my failings to shiftlessness, egoism, craziness, or not wanting to change. None of those are true," wrote one woman.

"My woman doesn't accept my ADHD and thinks I'm faking it. She says it's a reason to explain my failures, "said one hubby." My mate still does not understand that I'm not doing this on purpose. I try to get the effects right, but she ignores my trouble. I suppose my ADHD is a gift — I love how I am, and I can not change presently for her."

Forty-two percent of grown-ups with ADHD reported that their complaint gets in the way of their coitus life. Numerous say ADHD affects their focus during closeness" My mind wanders during coitus. It's hard to stay focused enough for coitus to be pleasurable for me." Some report that their ADHD mistakes outside the bedroom dampen closeness in bed" I've been a big letdown to my woman. I am not always apprehensive of what I must do, yet I don't particularly appreciate being mothered. I need closeness to feel loved, but my woman does not want to have coitus with a child. I do not condemn her."

ADHD mates say that having different bedtimes limits the quantum of coitus in some marriages." The problem is getting to bed beforehand enough that we are not both exhausted because my brain always wants to do one other thing."

The drug affects closeness, too. Some check libido; others fail to work through the evening hours." My goad drug wears off in the evening, making me perverse. I do not indeed want to be touched."

There are ADHD mates who are happy with their closeness, still." We have a healthy coitus life. I suppose ADHD makes coitus.

PART 2
Accepting

"I am my own biggest critic. Before anyone else has criticized me, I have already criticized myself. But for the rest of my life, I am going to be with me and I don't want to spend my life with someone who is always critical. So I am going to stop being my own critic. It's high time that I accept all the great things about me."

C. JoyBell C.

Chapter 6
Embrace Your Uniqueness

You Are Different

Grown-ups living with ADHD means to have peculiar neurology, which affects you pervasively and deeply. Specifics can help, but there's no cure. I recommend you learn to understand, accept and embrace your ADHD. By virtually addressing ADHD problems, one can live a fulfilled, successful and happy life. Hopefully, as you come to appreciate the positives in ADHD and the negative traits, you may not want treatment.

Live your ADHD life Aligned With Who You Are

Understanding your ADHD is fundamental to gaining control of your ADHD. So read books, web spots, and magazines; observe yourself and others at support groups; hear to your reference professionals, especially psychiatrists, and figure out how ADHD affects you. Everyone with ADHD has different challenges and strengths, so come as an expert in your ADHD.

Understanding means mending low tone regard after times of review; understanding means gaining new perceptivity into what may eventually work for you, and most importantly, understanding means a new stopgap.

Accepting and Embracing your ADHD

There are two sensible opinions to make about our ADHD challenges and issues.

We can:

· Accept that we've got a problem and find an ADHD-friendly approach or strategy to overcome or manage it.

· Accept we struggle with commodity, decide to live with it, and stop fussing and beating ourselves over it.

The option of floundering with an issue, doing nothing about it, and constantly feeling frustrated and unhappy with yourself – doesn't make sense. It leads to a lower tone- of regard, depression, and loathing.

I'm ADHD; I work on acceptance of my challenges. I now have an explanation for being wearied and emotional late due to my genes and dopamine. A reason isn't an excuse, so I concoct strategies to overcome my challenges and accept my limitations.

Focus on how to make effects more intriguing, develop and exploit being habits, award yourself, find easier ways to start tasks and spark yourself, and produce the routines and practices to keep doing them.

The drug business is to identify and define illness and give symptom operation with specifics and remedies. ADHD traits can make a living in the moment's world delicate, with the growing love of order, routine, and process. ADHD brings "co-morbidities" like depression, anxiety, and dependence. Problems can do at work, at home, with musketeers and family. It's excellent that croakers are involved in helping people with ADHD to give medical position support, but this doesn't make them experts in living a happy ADHD life.

ADHD is an inheritable difference, nearly as inherited as height. As altitudinous people are at the end of the height diapason, ADHD minds are at one end of an attention diapason. Being veritably altitudinous can bring problems, nasty tails, and banged facades on low door frames. Still, height brings benefits, too, like seeing over people's heads at musicals and being good at basketball. However, the medical profession and exploration would only concentrate on forepart injuries, not basketball chops, if height was unnoticeable, just as with ADHD, where all the focus is on negative traits and none on our creativity or humor. When you switch on the television and see the celebrities, the entrepreneurs, the jesters, the successful people so putatively ADHD, it's clear that concentrating on the negative traits of ADHD is absurd.

It's going to sound ordinary and indeed new to you to understand that many successful people, marketers, and those who deserve esteem and an air of mystery had acute ADHD diagnoses. Some of that distinction sucks; however, no longer all. If you have ADHD, you are different. Focus on where your differences are strengths and where your pursuits lie.

Alternate the context of your lifestyle to suit higher and how you use earlier than you attempt to alternate yourself to fit your context. Medicine can assist, but if the task is stupid and soulless, meds received restore that. If the job is lousy and dull, discover changing your activity before you recall medication.

Embrace your ADHD, experience being the greater emotional, forgetful, herbal, funny, intuitive, inspirational, procrastinating, unplanned, passionate ADHD you. Discern your hobbies and strengths, and cognizance your efforts there. Keep away from existence in that you strive not to be ADHD; discover one wherein you can have ADHD, be yourself, do what comes clearly, and do what you are enthusiastic about and engaged by using. In quick, embody your ADHD.

Chapter 7
Emotions and Sensitivity with ADHD

Social Confidence: How ADHD Affects Interpersonal Relationships

nterpersonal relationships outline and satisfy us. However, for folks with ADHD, our symptoms can negatively affect our buddies and spouses. At the same time, as we recognize how ADHD can affect our capability to cognizance, bear in mind, and get things finished, we do not often communicate about ADHD's effect on our capacity to develop and maintain connections –– and that needs to change.

When you are diagnosed with ADHD, medical doctors tell you that the condition will compromise your potential to complete responsibilities, that it will make it challenging to don't forget things and pay interest, and that it will result in blurting out matters that must in no way see the mild of day.

We understand those ADHD signs and symptoms can affect our process performance, our likeliness to get in an automobile wreck, and our ability to remember dates (after thirteen years, I forgot my husband's birthday this year — once more). However, what tends to be left behind is the recognition of how those signs affect our interpersonal relationships — people with significant others, coworkers, friends, and our kids.

Impulsivity and Romantic Relationships with ADHD

Negative impulse manipulation makes any relationship challenges. It impairs the capability to discern a special romantic relationship from a dangerous one.

Usually, the terrible boy appeared to laugh more at me in college than the good man did. Impulsive selections make it hard to live a terrific dating — or to get out of a horrific one.

Research recommends that people with ADHD are divorced greater regularly than people without it and that they remarry greater. It makes you feel: you have more significant divorces while your impulsivity leads you to pick improper companions or while you walk out too quickly on a terrific one.

Indeed, one of my ex-boyfriends (additionally with ADHD) and I almost ended up married in Vegas. We weren't even 21. We didn't care if the concept became excellent or wrong; it seemed amusing. Most straightforward, a nicely-timed cellphone name from a degree-headed professor talked us out of it.

Emotional regulation and Spiraling Reactions with ADHD

Adults with ADHD have trouble taming their moods. Nobody desires to be around someone who's constantly irritated. While we're indignant, we say things we remorse later. We're effortlessly overwhelmed via anger, and we can't disguise it. This may carry harsh results in paintings. We are easily overcome with rage and cannot mask it. This can lead to difficult results. Arguing with your boss is not a good idea and could have dire consequences. And even if you keep calm in front of your boss, you may channel anger towards coworkers or others like your spouse or baby.

When you have ADHD, there's additionally a good threat. You spend lots of your time feeling now not accurate, excellent, or guilty approximately things that aren't your fault. You have got what's known as rejection-sensitive dysphoria (RSD).

When my husband asks me to do an easy task, I will spiral: He isn't asking me to take out the garbage. He's saying, "Why haven't you taken the garbage out already? Why do you by no means take out the garbage?" honestly, he's asking for assistance with an easy task. However, I examine it as judging my conduct — and locating it wanting. I freak out and freeze up.

This may additionally happen while your boss makes tips about a way to improve your performance at work. You don't listen to constructive criticism; you pay attention, "You aren't desirable enough, and allow me to inform you the motives why." You hear it as an insult. You are green with envy; your boss is baffled.

Forgetfulness results in Inadvertently losing touch

There is some other trouble with ADHD and relationships: we're horrible long-distance friends. We don't name vintage buddies as it doesn't arise to us — out of sight, out of mind.

We are afraid that we don't have anyone from beyond, that we can't hold onto humans, and that no person cares about us. However, it's now not that humans don't care. It's that we overlook to reach out, and, after some time, our friends forestall trying. They forget us as we ignore them.

One in every one of my exceptional pals from high faculty unfriended me on FB. She didn't imply to. But she didn't realize I'd changed my married call and commenced using a nickname on my profile. One more great relationship is down the drain. And what's more, RSD makes it impossible to attain out again.

Medical doctors and researchers need to talk more approximately how ADHD affects relationships. A planner and a fidget spinner assist with my ADHD. But what might help greater is therapy specializing in personal relationships and the minefield they pose for people with the situation.

ADHD, Women, and the Danger of Emotional Withdrawal

The need to get away from society and to tend to isolate oneself is something that those with ADHD certainly experience in their life. ADHS and removal go hand in hand. Numerous women with ADHD learn from a continuance of rejection, disappointment, and bullying. Breaking this unhealthy habit is a complex and delicate process, but you need to understand how this affects your relationships. When your partner, your husband, talks but you don't listen to him, you are rejecting him.

What is he talking about? They are trivial, everyday things: doing the laundry, taking the children to school, or simply hanging the clothes.

My husband keeps talking, but I'm not listening.

I am turning him down. You see, my ADHD and emotional withdrawal stem from my perceptiveness of rejection, or rejection sensitive dysphoria (RSD), which can lead me to misinterpret my human being as horrible and ephemeral.

The stew of guilt and wrathfulness, shame and misery can be overpowering. So I turn down. I coil into myself, cut myself off emotionally. I know it's not a healthy managing medium. But at times, it's the only bone.

The emotional pullout is a Learned geste

Girls with ADHD frequently learn emotional pullout at a youthful age ADHD, and emotional escape often comes hand-in-hand for women.

We are daydreamy and spacey, infrequently anchored forcefully in the then and now(presumably because the then and now means forgotten papers, missed deadlines, and people demanding we did not do better). Our disorganization can make us a social leper as other scholars seek to part themselves from the" wrong" sprat. We can sluggishly pick up on other girls' social cues with ease. We frequently blurt out impulsively at unhappy times, which can, as others have refocused, attract the attention of a bully.

So, as if social acceptance by "bad girls" wasn't enough, girls with ADHD often find themselves painfully bullied and, in the 1980s and 1990s, none.

He did a lot about it other than telling us to stink. However, some "genius" was also able to make the usual comparisons that if it were a boy who was bullied, no one would be shocked. But this is just one way of setting the stage for muddying the waters and shifting attention to something else, making girls with ADHD increasingly lonely and vulnerable.

Frequently, we were our only supporters. Our preceptors and parents might have dismissed our complaints as tattling or brushed them off — as mine did with a commodity like," If you learned to act like everyone differently, this wouldn't be to you." We knew to condemn ourselves for our acceptance; we were not good at class in the social groups or the fashionability other scholars enjoyed.

So we cut ourselves off. We have learned not to look because loving hurts too much. We retreated inward when the teasing started, when the bullying started (again) and when the spitballs flew. It was the only way we knew to deal with it, to handle it somehow.

And this heavy emotional burden that is ADHD accompanies us into adulthood when we become adult women.

As we have learned to dissociate ourselves from others, we develop other unhealthy management mechanisms. For this, we take refuge in emotional withdrawal, which involves bottling our feelings. It consists of cutting out people who might help us because we are so used to rejection that we have learned to anticipate it.

But what do the experts say? Here, studies have shown that we are still in it. Young puberty girls with ADHD are more likely to struggle with social, attention, and organizational difficulties, have lower self-esteem, experience more torture and brain impairment, and feel less in control of their lives. However, women with ADHD are about 2.5% more likely to fall into depression than women without ADHD.

These are enough dismal circumstances. And numerous of them stem from our need to" stuff" our feelings or shut down how we feel about managing the world around us. We are always hysterical about placing a bottom wrong, missing a social cue, or forgetting an important deadline. And all the itineraries in the world can not help us. We have learned to anticipate the constant attack, so we have developed unhealthy managing mechanisms, some of them blooming into full-bloated psychiatric diseases to serve in a neurotypical world.

This is why women who experience ADHD Withdrawal tend to alienate those around them. In a complicated way, they push away those who love them most because they do not want to be placed in front of themselves to dig deep. But also because, as a defense mechanism, it is sometimes useful not to have anyone to love or someone to love us in order not to be afraid of anything, not even losing those we love.

Again, the statistics are not on the side of people with ADHD, who experience twice the divorce rate of the general population. The reasons for a divorce are the most disparate, it is obvious. Still, it is easy to conclude that this difference may partly be due to the difficulties deriving from ADHD in the sexual sphere, from losing attention to everyday things, or simply from the incorrect and confusing management of the time.

Although a woman with ADHD and her partner are aware of so many difficulties, they can easily conclude that they feel unloved. And this is what should be avoided.

How Can We Address Emotional Withdrawal Appreciative?

1. Fete that you withdraw from people and situations as a managing medium. This can not be easy to admit since it's the only way you've fared for so long. But recognition is the first step. When you turn down from your partner or musketeers, learn to say," I'm turning down and entwining up in this situation. I'm shutting down." That takes a lot of serious work. It means you must step outdoors in your emotional responses and first realize what's going on. However," I'm emotionally withdrawing right now" is a significant first step in the right direction, If you succeed in saying it to yourself.
2. Take the(actually scary) step of articulating what is passing. It helps to study a script to go on with it. This can be commodity simple" I've ADHD. I learned to withdraw as a managing medium. When you did or said x, it made me feel like I've to start to cover myself." It does not mean that you do or do not have to retire. It means you're letting your mate (likely your partner) know what is passing. They will not feel they're to condemn because you've predicated it in your learned geste. And you can hopefully work on some consolation and help together.
3. Next, sit down and make a list. Rather than withdrawing, what would you rather have to be? Perhaps you'd rather have confirmation that your passions matter. Maybe you'd rather have the verbal assurance that you're loved just like you are. Perhaps you would like a hug. However, maybe you'd like to have your hand held instead If you cringe from

that or aren't ready for it. Communicate a whole list of actions on the part of your mate that could help you feel safer, and also partake in it with them. Do not condemn; offer constructive advice on how to help you with emotional disassociation.

Pursue Professional Help

We have seen that women who" stuff" their passions and suffer from sorrowfully unhappy emotional responses can be helical into a host of adverse issues. Are you in remedy right now? You should be.

Choosing a good cognitive behavioral therapist can help you develop more managing mechanisms to help you deal with your passions. You will learn to change your illogical study patterns – in this case, the idea that unstudied reflections or input from other people negate your tone- worth – to more positive bones and to manage when the negative studies arrive to deal with them, not posterity on them or stuff them.

When choosing a psychotherapist, you must pay attention to some essential things. What if you should see an ADHD trainer or therapist? Someone who offers CBT (cognitive behavioral remedy) or DBT (dialectical behavior therapy, a kind of CBT) is preferred, along with a specialization in treating ADHD. These professionals can help you manage your emotional side and the propensity to settle down through tools that will help you understand healthier and less dangerous management mechanisms that can improve your relationships rather than sabotage them.

The emotional pullout is a geste numerous women with ADHD have learned through a long life of rejection, fear, and bullying; it can take time, remedy, and help to get through it. Emotional pullouts can hurt your connections, destabilize your marriage, and sabotage your life through unhealthy managing mechanisms. But you can this web of mistrust and fear and, finally, feel free. An essential role in all this is played by the figures that rotate next to you; that is your support network: partner, therapist, and family.

But utmost of all, you need a solid commitment to change. Without that, you will be stuck in your old pullout pattern, which does not help anyone, least of all yourself.

The Gaslighting Threat for Women with ADHD

Gaslighters frequently target women and men with ADHD. Then's how to fete when you're psychologically or emotionally manipulated and how to shut down the abuse.

What Is Gaslighting?

Gaslighting is a form of cerebral or emotional abuse — a series of manipulative ways to gain control of another person. By blatantly and constantly lying or challenging reality, the gaslighters keep their victims off- fettle and make them question themselves. Numerous times, a person's opinion of ADHD is used against them by the gaslighter. I've been a therapist 20 times, and recently I've seen more and more guests with ADHD reporting being gaslighted in their connections and at their jobs.

Grown-ups with ADHD may be more vulnerable to gaslighting due to issues with tone- regard, difficulty with once connections, and passions of guilt and shame. One of the stylish defenses against gaslighting is to educate yourself about this kind of emotional abuse. Know that there's a stopgap, and you can rebuild your life after living with gaslighting for months or, indeed, times.

Gaslighting Behaviors

Gaslighters occasionally hide their mates' things and condemn their mates for being "reckless," "lazy," or "so ADHD" when they can't find the particulars. A gaslighter may also tell their mate that they don't need to take a drug for ADHD because "Nobody knows you better than me."

Gaslighting actions include

- Telling you that you didn't pay attention or you didn't see or hear something infidelity frequently, but obsessively criminating you of cheating
- Saying that other people suppose you're crazy
- Bending you against people(this is known as "triangulating") romanticizing you, also attenuating you, and eventually discarding the relationship

Why and How Gaslighters Target People with ADHD

Gaslighters smell vulnerabilities in a person. They specifically target people grieving a loss or feeling shy or isolated. You may have been accused of being a particular or complex type. However, you presumably grew up feeling "lower than, If you have ADHD." You may have had difficulties maintaining gemütlichkeit or connections.

When you meet a manipulator for the first time, you must pay attention to what is called a "love bomb." You will hear everything you want to say, so you can feel accepted for who you are. Once you have fallen into his trap here, he goes on the attack.

Beforehand, the gaslighter asks you about your fears and crunches. It feels good to have someone harkening to you and minding what you have to say. Still, the gaslighter is gathering data for security against you. You may ultimately hear, "No wonder your family doesn't talk to you presently. She knows you're crazy, too."

A typical manipulative attitude is to become meek when you tend to push it away. This is because they want to regain their control over you and your life, so they will let your friends and family know that they miss you and might make a crazy gesture if you don't return to them. They will apologize for what happened but maybe "only" for the tones used, not for their content; a manipulator is convinced that he is right and not wrong. Either way, they will promise never to do it again; needless to say that this promise will obviously be awaited, and indeed his behavior will worsen.

How to Escape Gaslighting In a Relationship

For utmost people, leaving a gaslighting relationship means" no contact — at each." Block phone numbers and dispatch addresses. Tell buddies and family that you will not hear of any dispatches transferred. It would be wish if you also met with a pukka internal health professional; having ADHD makes you vulnerable to anxiety and mood conditions. Plan and follow through with an ADHD treatment plan, and establish connections with the healthy people in your life. Still, meet with an attorney to develop a detailed parenting plan; if you have children with a gaslighter

Gaslighting at the Workplace

Occasionally heads and associates take advantage of the fact that someone has ADHD. They will charge you for being absentminded or not minding your work.

Ask your master or colleague to shoot you a dispatch with instructions or details of an assignment. However, relate to that dispatch, somewhat condemning yourself, If you complete the task and are told that you didn't do what was asked.

Talking About Mental Health in Your Relationship

Talking about your internal health with a loved one can help you gain power over yourself and the world. It's an occasion to make a robust support system and foster deeper connections in your connections. But talking about internal health can be delicate, especially if you've no way to open up about it.

How can you initiate exchanges about internal health without feeling shamefaced or awkward? It might feel uncomfortable at first. The key is to make sure you consider your loved one's perspective. Your significant other or loved one isn't your therapist, but they can be essential to your internal health support system.

Try these tips when talking about internal health.

Still, do a quick palpitation check with yourself to prepare for a healthier and further productive discussion, If it's your first time opening up about your internal health with a loved one. Here are some tips to keep helpful start opening up to someone or starting a conversation:

Not everyone can talk about internal health.

1. Paper the following questions: Who is this person for you? Does he make you feel comfortable? Are you vulnerable in his presence? How does this person behave towards your vulnerable being? Is it cozy?
2. Write your passions down first to organize your studies and gain a better perspective on the issue.

3. Set the tone for the discussion. Try to make this person understand what they represent and that you need to be transparent with them.
4. Avoid opening a river in flood; that is, try to be measured in sharing your situation; this sharing may be too much to endure all at once. Your goal is for her to feel overwhelmed by the circumstance.
5. Try to be straightforward and no-nonsense by addressing one topic at a time. Not everyone has the knowledge, empathy, and compassion to reuse the nuances of internal health.
6. Don't feel pressured or indebted to tell them anything you're not comfortable talking about yet.
7. Use the "I" statements to help reduce passions of guilt or blame. This way, your interlocutor will know that you are referring to yourself and will not feel called into question or criticized for anything.
8. Use examples. When explaining internal health conditions or symptoms, provide specific cases to help them understand what it is like. For example, "even the most mundane daily activities can be difficult to do when my symptoms are severely acute."
9. Take the advice the interlocutor gives you and listen to him while he talks to you without prejudice. Exchanges are bilateral, so listening to the other person is vital. You can't control how other people respond, but you can control how you answer and talk.
10. Thank them for their time. Let them know how appreciative you're for them taking the time to hear.

Opening up to professionals about your internal health, partake in your story with an internal health provider. If you find it delicate talking about internal health with the people close to you. Endured internal health providers understand internal health complications and can help you find possible results.

The benefits of internal health exchanges

Talking about internal health in your connections is an instigative and courageous step. These exchanges can help your loved bones

understand the specifics of your symptoms or passions or ease their enterprises by making them more apprehensive of what's passing in your life.

Having internal health exchanges with people you trust can also help you in other areas of life.

Start opening up about your internal health with your loved ones to help make a robust support system – because no bone

should deal with their inner health struggles alone.

How to Balance Between your Mental Health and Relationships

Married with ADHD: How Real Couples Make It Work

When we learn of a married couple in which one spouse has been diagnosed with ADHD - we generally hear about the problems that the non-ADHD partner has to face: not being able to calculate on their partner to get the effects, forgetfulness, impulsiveness, important feelings and anger that hang over the relationship. But what is the other side of the coin? What challenges and difficulties, and good feelings that ADHD partners experience? How and how does ADHD affect love and marriage? How do you live in a marriage where there is a third wheel that is ADHD?

More than 700 adults with ADHD have talked about their relationships and relationship problems; for example, they have expressed what they would like to change, improve, or wish for their future. The results were surprising, occasionally funny, and often reassuring.

Mates diagnosed with ADHD share numerous of the same frustrations as their non-ADHD counterparts.

Mostly they feel not understood, not considered, and not love; therefore, they tend to have fits of anger if their mates blame them if the relationship goes downhill. But they feel guilty when their relationship breaks down because they fear, and perhaps sometimes it does, that it is due to their inability to focus on a goal or their disorganization.

But primarily, mates with ADHD are faithful spouses; they take marriage as seriously as family and relationship. They try to react when things are not going well, improve their health, and learn more about ADHD and potential treatment options.

Many of the interviewees reported that, after a few difficult years, they were able to put together effective relationship strategies.

TRUE STORY: Sarah and her husband were married for two years when she was diagnosed with ADHD. She never received treatment and decided to begin stimulant therapy after a long period of reflection.

"When I was diagnosed with ADHD, it was like a bolt from the blue for me, but at that moment, just as after the storm, the sky cleared: I finally put the puzzle pieces together."

I was afraid to talk about it with my husband, but my happiness was too much; I wanted to make him understand how much I finally felt I had a place in the world.

He did not understand at first, but after taking an interest in the symptoms and the disease, he helped me decide to start therapy.

A partner supporting you in this long process is essential because you have a shoulder to lean on when it all seems insurmountable."

"My ADHD is still here, the third wheel in our marriage, but now we know it, my husband has realized that it is not that I do not watch anything. He understands that my brain can't stop because it's everywhere."

Communication Difficulties

Of the more than 700 adults with ADHD surveyed, most said communication difficulties were the biggest obstacle in relationships.

Often you feel belittled and are not always able to show attention to something.

Said another woman with ADHD, "I have a problem recycling what he says if there's a lot of noise going on and he's in another room. Occasionally I don't hear him at each because I've drifted off into chaos and don't realize it."

Other common problems reported were wrathfulness and outbursts, to the point of screaming and crying.

Utmost of the repliers reported unintentional communication problems with their mates. "Especially in the evening, my studies are arbitrary, and I'll impulsively say effects out loud. My mate is caught off guard and hurt by my reflections," Jack wrote.

Sharing Mental Load: A Pick for Empowering Women with ADHD

It is known that the mental burden regarding household chores, house management, and children (if any) are tasks that, unfortunately, fall on women, regardless of whether or not they have been diagnosed with ADHD.

This aspect is more remarkable in some areas of the country where the perception of women is antiquated and determined by a male-dominated and patriarchal society from which we women should be able to free ourselves by fighting.

Feminism helps us because it puts the human being at the center. The woman becomes a subject and no longer an object, a woman capable of expressing her needs and being listened to, because she is as important as her spouse.

Things may go differently in families where the woman with ADHD or does not cohabits with a female partner, but there is insufficient evidence to support this hypothesis.

Using reflection on this aspect will help women understand if their partner respects them as human beings without expecting the impossible from them and giving nothing in return. Reciprocity is fundamental for the serenity of women with ADHD, as feminism is for the empowerment of all women worldwide.

Adults with ADHD said they managed more than half of all ménage tasks; 11 percent do it all. Men diagnosed with ADHD share parenting, but their time is limited by work, or they cultivate other areas of their life.

Nora and her husband have been married for ten years and have two children with special needs. "Until we had children, I was fit to keep him together," Nora said. "But now I can't negotiate anything! (My husband) will say: 'Why can't you send the washing machine?' She acts like she is my father, not my husband. "

According to Nora, her husband has made her life impossible because he is so caught up in the deadline "to-do list" that it makes her feel even more inadequate.

That's why after two years of marriage, she started using drugs. Cocaine stimulates her to be more focused but makes her seem as if reality were different.

She knows that sooner or later, she will have to give up on us, but for now, it's her only way to deal with the pain of how her husband makes her feel human.

She knows that sooner or later, she will have to give up on us, but for now, it's her only way to deal with the pain of how her husband makes her feel human.

The risk in their couple now is mostly about divorce.

This is why they decided to undertake a couple of therapy paths; both want to avoid this hypothesis; after all, they love each other with their strengths and weaknesses.

"It's All My Fault"

Many women with ADHD believe they are the cause of all the problems in their relationships.

The negative image they have of themselves turns out to be one of the most depressing things about ADHD, and they feel they don't deserve their partner.

In fact, they often don't feel smart enough; they believe they have tricked their partner into marrying or living with a person with a "normal brain," to name a few statements from women with ADHD.

The most terrible thing is that they do not find anything positive in having ADHD and not be able to do anything good to the relationship; indeed, they identify themselves with their brain disorder. Thus they think that there is nothing positive in themselves or in the peculiarity of living with this brain disorder.

Light at the End of the Tunnel

However, some positives that ADHD has brought to their relationships have emerged.

There are three particular things that people with ADHD know well:

- Spontaneity
- Hyperfocus
- Creativity

These characteristics are very useful in a relationship because spontaneity is able to make everything lighter, to make impulse decisions as if it were the last day of your life.

Living in the present is easier sometimes.

Hyperfocus along with creativity are two qualities that help the relationship take off, as when the person with ADHD is hyperfocused, he focuses on the partner who consequently feels important.

Creativity is a positive trait for an ADHD spouse. Respondents say that creativity makes everyday life and special occasions interesting.

TRUE STORY - A Dream Relationship!

True Story: Jessica and her husband have been together for 25 years. She was diagnosed with ADHD 8 months ago.

"The diagnosis opened a world to me: before, I often thought I didn't do the simplest things right, like drying glasses. After my diagnosis, I was able to tell my husband that I didn't want to do it as he did."

One thing ADHD taught me was when to recognize that you need help and be able to ask for it. Now my husband knows what's behind my silence or request, and I don't feel I have to or want to face everything alone.

No doubt, discovering that I have ADHD has dramatically improved our life as a couple; now, I notice the positive things my mind allows me to see.

The medicines have helped me a lot. Now and then, I tend to get distracted again or interrupt him while he speaks, but I immediately notice the mistake, and we often laugh at it together.

I knew I had something different, but I realized there was nothing wrong with me; I decided to live my life in my way, and as the saying goes, "the exceptional feat is to be normal"!

The Need to Be Meticulous and Perfectionist

Why Women with ADHD Are frequently Perfectionists?

Numerous women acquired tone- regard through early academic successes. As grown-ups, they still calculate intellect to help them compensate, but the difficulty of sustaining attention makes them question their capacities. The road to success now requires tremendous sacrifice in both time and energy. The eternal confrontation with colleagues or other people who do not seem to struggle from the outside is difficult; we must try not to let any emotion shine through. Still, rigid perfectionism comes at a high price. Grim tone- monitoring is fueled by exhausting anxiety. Some women stay up utmost of the night immersed in compulsive medications. But when commodity falls through the cracks, their high norms leave them feeling dissipated and undeserving of compassion. Their façade is only successful if no bone suspects the despair that consumes them. Still, this mask of conformity noway allows them to be known; their struggles are secret but no less dangerous.

Our tips to improve your life as a couple:

- Accept yourself;
- Follow the therapy;
- Accept that you need help;
- Approach feminism to improve self-esteem as a woman.

Chapter 8
Working balance with ADHD

A long workday increases stress; experts tell us that work-related stress damages our brain and our social life.

It is important to find a balance between private life and work; the usual question "live to work or work to live?"

There is no answer because it depends on our personal scale of values: friends, family, work, and free time.

All the more reason, women with ADHD find it even more difficult to carry on a situation of work balance precisely because other spheres can suffer imbalances.

But a changing balance is possible. You just need to listen to yourself, see the space you need and set some boundaries to get there. Boundaries have a lot of power as they can determine the health of our relationships, whether or not we achieve our pretensions, and indeed our happiness. But healthy boundaries aren't always easy to identify or apply. Consider these five ways to perfect work-life balance by setting boundaries hear to how you feel.

To define the space you need, you have to figure out why you need to set those boundaries. And that means relating your passions. A big part of ADHD remedy is learning emotional mindfulness. Why? Because the ADHD brain gets fluently consumed and hooked by its feelings. In fact, ADHDers frequently witness all feelings intensively- – indeed evanescent feelings. This can beget struggles with emotional regulation. These feelings can beget prolonged spells of wrathfulness, fear, and avoidance, in addition to perceptivity to review or rejection(also known as rejection-sensitive dysphoria, or RSD).

Tuning into how you're feeling can get you in touch with your requirements and objects. For illustration, are you working late because of a fear of getting fired or because you suppose your master will be frenetic at you (despite the lack of substantiation for both)? Getting in touch with your passions can help you check them against the data so you can decide whether acting on a feeling is really in your stylish interest.

Need help naming passions? Start with these five fear, wrathfulness, guilt/shame, sadness, and happiness.

Practice tone- care by knowing your value.

Tone care isn't all bubble cataracts and faces masks. Tone-care can mean understanding what you value and setting boundaries to support those values. Adding tone- care thresholds with perfecting tone- worth. It's common enough for grown-ups with ADHD to struggle with a strong inner critic – – that little voice saying you're not good enough. Turns out a continuance of review for unintended miscalculations can take its risk. Still, we can decide the energy – – positive or negative – – that we bring into our lives. And we've power over our tone- worth. It would be useful to identify your Jiminy Cricket and also thank him for his time, but agree to disagree.

How to Figure Out the Structure of Your Diurnal Life

It's important to make systems that produce structure in your everyday life. We frequently spend a lot of energy fussing about effects because our brain is motioning an early alert/ warning system about systems that don't work for us. Because ADHD impacts administrative functioning, time operation is a skill that most grown-ups with ADHD struggle with.

Learning says "NO."

What is the most beautiful word in the English language which, for the utmost of us, is also the hardest to say?

"NO"

It is worth it for ADHD women to learn how to use this word more often than they usually do.

We can not always say no; that would be too rigid a boundary. But a well-placed no can make a world of difference.

Start small. You were maybe saying no thresholds with not responding to a textbook, saying no to feasts, or babysitting for a friend when you'd instead catch up on Netflix. Saying no to more significant effects will probably work out better if you have some experience saying no to the lower results.

Get clear on your values.

Values make boundaries clear. For illustration, you don't have grief without connection or social anxiety without minding about relationships. Still, our conduct doesn't always align with what we watch about. Value explanation is the key to carrying a rich and meaningful life. For illustration, if you value family but work 80 hours a week, there might be a dissociation between your values and your conduct.

We have some good news: the chosen values are not self-excluding; they can easily coexist. Our choices determine them.

Our daily decisions, day by day, define our values. For example, if we realize that we are on a diet, we can order a light poke bowl and decide to celebrate our birthday.

We do not have a detailed vision of the future but live the present by choosing our values to choose ourselves daily.

4 Tips For Better Work Life-Balance

Work-life balance is different for everyone, but health and career experts offer tips on how to find the right balance for you.

1. Let Go of Perfectionism

Numerous overachievers develop perfectionistic tendencies at a young age when the demands on their time are limited to school, pursuits, and perhaps an after-school job. As a sprat, it's easier to maintain this perfectionist habit, but as you grow up, life gets more complicated. As you advance up the career ladder and your family grows, your obligations become greater. Perfectionism becomes unattainable, and this habit can be destructive if left unchecked.

Perfectionism is an enemy: it paves the way to burnout. As life expands, "niit's very difficult, both neurologically and psychologically, to maintain the habit of perfection," she says, adding that striving for excellence rather than perfection is healthier.

2. Open

Technology helped our lives to be easier in many ways, from telecommuting to programs that make our jobs easier. But it has also created the prospect of constant accessibility. The workday never seems to end." There are times when you should turn off your phone and enjoy the moment, is what expert usually says: phone messages disrupt your free time and give you a lot of stress. So the advice is not to text your sprat's soccer game or write work emails while you are with your family. It's essential to develop good quality time habits by turning off email, phone, etc. Flexible people have less control over their lives, while reactive people have less power and are more prone to stress.

3. Exercise and Meditate

Vital things in life such as eating, breathing, sleeping, or going to the bathroom are the necessary action we make when we are busy. We need to add practice and exercise. Even when we are busy, we quit it off.

Exercise is an effective stress reliever. It pumps beneficial endorphins through your body. It lifts your mood and can do a one-two punch by putting you in a more meditative state, according to the Mayo Clinic.

Powder York recommends taking plenty of time each week to tone up, whether through exercise, yoga, or contemplation. You can start with small things: deep breathing exercises during your commute, a short, five-nanosecond contemplation session, or replacing bad habits like smoking or drinking with a healthier form of stress relief.

"When I talk about balance, it does not all have to come down to completing and accomplishing a task, but also tone care so that the body, mind, and spirit are refreshed," says Puder- York.

Exercise and calm-down go hand-in-hand, and not just at the moment. The key is to find something you can incorporate into your life to stimulate your parasympathetic nervous system," Robinson says. Short, thoughtful exercises like deep breathing or resting your senses in your present environment are excellent places to start. These exercises involve little effort but offer significant nets. Over time, you'll find that your parasympathetic nervous system begins to trump your sympathetic nervous system in your life."

4. Limit time-wasting conditioning and people.

First, determine what is most important in your life. This list will look different for everyone, so make sure it reflects your priorities. Next, fix your boundaries so you can devote the correct amount of time to your priorities.

But also set rules that will keep you in line when work or surfing the web sends you into a time frenzy. Try productivity software like Freedom or LeechBlock if you mindlessly surf Facebook or cat blogs when you should be working. And if you find your time being taken up by less influential people, find ways to limit those relationships diplomatically. Are you cornered by a chatterbox in the office every morning? Do you have a drink with your colleagues the night before a busy day at work? Apologize politely.

PART 3
Acting

"Action has magic, grace and power in it."
"The moment one definitely commits oneself, then Providence moves, too. All sorts of things occur to help one that would never have otherwise occurred...unforeseen incidents and meetings and material assistance, which no man could have dreamed would have come his way."

JOHANN WOLFGANG VON GOETHE

Chapter 9

Supplementation and Diet for ADHD Women

How Nutrition Harmonizes the ADHD Brain

Complex carbohydrates, omega- 3 adipose acids, extra protein, and specific vitamins help our brain cells perform their functions efficiently and effectively. In an ADHD brain, these nutrients can be STRONG. Find out how!

Exploration shows that what you feed your body directly correlates to how your brain processes. Diet and nutrition impact cognition, attention, mood, and sleep. According to the Harvard Health Blog, people who eat" clean" or" whole" refections high in vegetables, fruits, undressed grains, and spare flesh are more likely to witness the best emotional health.

Can perfect eating help combat symptoms of ADHD?

Grown-ups and parents of children with ADHD are chancing that, while whole foods may not be a cure, **changes in what you eat** can make a big difference in some cases. **Nutrition and ADHD** go hand-in-hand.

Poor eating habits don't beget ADHD. And when it comes to controlling inattention, impulsivity, and other symptoms, there's no cover for drug and behavioral remedies, which are the most effective approaches and the only bones recommended by the **American Academy of Pediatrics**.

Still, grown-ups and parents of children with attention poverties have long reported a connection between the foods they eat and their geste and symptoms. Now, wisdom is beginning to add credence to those compliances.

Exploration shows that protein promotes alertness in the brain. Carbohydrates do the contrary. And artificial colors and flavors are indeed worse, which may explain why Fruity Pebbles are one of the worst breakfasts for your child.

In substance, the better you want your brain to perform, the different undressed proteins, meals, vegetables, and fruits you should eat.

Different studies show a relationship between food and **ADHD symptoms**. One, published in PEDIATRICS in 2010, concluded that fungicides, specifically organophosphates, set up on fruits and vegetables might be linked to ADHD. The more advanced the situations of the composites detected in a child's urine, the more likely they're to be diagnosed with ADHD. The secret? Eat organic, suggest the study's authors. Another study, published in the diseases in 2010, showed that a Western diet reused flesh, fast foods, high-fat dairy products, and sticky foods doubled the threat of ADHD compared with a good diet.

Nutrition Affects the ADHD Brain in Different Ways

1. Like other cells in the body, the brain needs proper nutrition to perform its functions.
2. The myelin jacket, which covers the axons of brain cells, as sequestration protects electrical cables, needs the cor-

rect situations of nutrients to speed the transmission of the electrical signals between brain cells.

3. Neurotransmitters — dopamine, serotonin, and norepinephrine — also depend on diet for proper performance.

Suppose the proper **nutrients** are not accessible to the brain, and its circuits miscarry.

Carbohydrates and ADHD Brain Powerful

Carbohydrates affect brain function and personal mood. The sugar rate from a particular food is called the "glycemic indicator." Foods with a high glycemic indicator stimulate the pancreas to cache high insulin situations, which causes sugar to empty snappily from the blood into the cells. Insulin regulates the ups and campo of blood sugar and the rollercoaster geste that occasionally goes with them. Low-glycemic foods deliver a steady force of sugar, helping a person with ADHD control geste and ameliorate performance.

Foods with stylish brain sugars include

Fruits, grapefruit, apples, cherries, oranges, and grapes. Fruits have a lower GI (glycemic indicator) than fruit authorities because fruit fiber slows fruit sugar immersion. An apple is more brain cells-friendly than apple juice; an orange is better than an orange juice. Please note that the acid in orange, **grape** and their **authorities** interrupts the immersion of short- amusement goad **ADHD specifics** and should be avoided when taking these conventions.

Cereals and grains oatmeal, bran, advanced-fiber cereals, and pasta also have low GI. sludge flakes and sugarcoated **breakfast** cereals have advanced Civilians and should be avoided.

Vegetables and legumes, like soybeans, order sap, and lentils, have the smallest GI of any food.

Dairy products Milk and yogurt have low Civilians, slightly advanced like legumes but lower than fresh fruits. Yogurt has a lower glycemic indicator than yogurt, with fruit preserves or sugar added.

Protein and ADHD Brain Power

The brain makes a variety of chemical couriers, or neurotransmitters, to regulate insomnia and sleep. Studies by Massachusetts Institute of Neuroscientist Richard WurtmanPh.D. and others have shown that protein triggers alertness- converting neurotransmitters, while carbohydrates spark doziness.

These findings support the widespread belief that people with ADHD do better after eating a **protein-rich breakfast** and lunch. Yet child psychologist VincentJ. Monastra, CEO of an ADHD clinic in New York, says that of the 500 children a time he evaluates for ADHD, lower than 5 percent are eating the government-recommended quantities of protein at breakfast and lunch. In addition to boosting alert, says Monastra, a protein-rich breakfast seems to reduce the liability that ADHD drugs will beget perversity or restlessness.

Proteins affect brain performance by furnishing the amino acids from which **neurotransmitters** are made. Neurotransmitters are biochemical couriers that carry signals from one brain cell to another. The better you feed these couriers, the more efficiently and directly they deliver the goods, allowing your ADHD child to be alert at the academy or you to be more on top of effects at work.

Two amino acids, tryptophan and tyrosine, are essential structure blocks of neurotransmitters. These amino acids impact the four principal neurotransmitters — serotonin, made from the amino acid tryptophan, epinephrine, norepinephrine, and dopamine, made from the amino acid tyrosine. Tryptophan is an essential amino acid. The body doesn't make it; the diet must supply it. The body can make tyrosine if there isn't enough in the diet.

"Because the body makes brain awakening neurotransmitters when you eat proteins, start your day with a breakfast that includes protein," says **Laura Stevens,** a nutritionist at Purdue University and author of 14 EFFECTIVE WAYS TO HELP YOUR ADHD CHILD. "Also, look for ways to slip in spare protein during the day."

"Protein helps keep blood sugar situations steady and prevents the internal declines that come from eating a mess containing too numerous simple carbs," says **Ned Hallowell, M.D.**, author of DRIVEN TO DISTRACTION.

Still, suppose your family's breakfast idea is toast, sticky cereals, or doughnuts. In that case, you do not need to eat a plate of eggs and bacon every morning to meet your daily protein conditions." We are not talking about a ton of food," says Monastra, author of Parenthood CHILDREN ADHD 10 Assignments THAT MEDICINE CAN NOT Educate.

Depending on their age, children need between 25 to 31 grams of protein a day. Grown-ups need 45 to 70 grams. You can get 7 grams in a mug of milk or soy milk, one egg, or an ounce of rubbish or meat.

The 5 Balanced Breakfasts

Nutrition packed breakfast should contain a balance of complex carbohydrates and protein.

Suppose grains, plus dairy, plus fruits.

1. Granola cereal, yogurt, sliced apple
2. Climbed eggs, wholegrain toast, orange
3. Veggie omelet, fresh fruit with yogurt, bran muffin
4.
5. Wholegrain flapjacks or hotcakes outgunned with berries and yogurt, milk
6. low-fat rubbish melted on wholegrain toast, pear, etc.

"Fats make up 65% of the brain and the jitters that run every system in the body," says William Sears, an associate clinical professor at the University of California. "The better fat in the diet, the better the brain will serve."

The most important brain functions are the two essential adipose acids in **fish oil** painting linoleic (omega 6) and nascence-linolenic (**omega 3**). These are the high structural factors of brain cell membranes and an essential part of the enzymes that permits cell membranes to transport nutrients in and out of cells. Western diets contain too numerous omega- 6 adipose acids and too many omegala- 3s, which are set up in cold-water fish(primarily salmon and tuna), soybeans, walnuts, wheat origin, pumpkin seeds, and eggs. Flaxseed and canola canvases are good sources of omega 3s.

"Individualities with ADHD who have low situations of omega 3s will show the biggest enhancement in internal focus and cognitive function when they add further of these healthy fats to their diet," says Richard Brown, clinical professor of psychiatry at Columbia University College

Vitamins and ADHD Brain Power

Studies indicate that children in grade academies whose diets are supplemented with applicable vitamins and minerals scored more advanced on intelligence tests than those who took no supplements. This is good news, but it comes with a critical caveat that inheritable abnormalities similar to MTHFR can make some accessories delicate and dangerous. Therefore, you should always consult your croaker before introducing a new vitamin or supplement to your or your child's diet. Indeed the putatively inoffensive vitamin B can beget grave side goods in specific individualities.

Then are some specific vitamins and minerals affect geste and literacy in children and grown-ups.

The brain requires vitamin C to make neurotransmitters. The brain has a unique vitamin c" pump," which draws redundant vitamin c out of the blood into the brain.

Vitamin B6 insufficiency causes perversity and fatigue. Acceptable situations of the vitamin increase the brain's conditions of the neurotransmitter dopamine, adding alertness.

Iron is also necessary for making dopamine. One small study showed ferritin situations to be low in 83 percent of children with ADHD, compared to 17 percent of a control group. Everyday iron situations relate to severe ADHD.

Zinc regulates dopamine neurotransmitters and may make methylphenidate more effective by perfecting the brain's response to dopamine Low situations of this mineral supplement with **inattention**.

Further of these nutrients isn't inescapably better and occasionally problematic. Studies using the megavitamin remedy in children with ADHD showed no effect.

What Not to Eat Food perceptivity and Elimination Diets

Studies show that perceptivity to certain foods may worsen symptoms of ADHD in children.

When placed on a special elimination diet banning foods that spark unwanted geste, as numerous as 30 percent of toddlers and preschoolers profit, says Eugene Arnold, M.D., author of *A Family's companion to attention- deficiency Hyperactivity* complaint and professor emeritus of psychiatry at Ohio State University. He says that such a diet doesn't affect grown-ups with ADD or ADHD.

On an elimination diet, you should eat only foods doubtful to beget responses:

* Lamb
* Chicken
* Potatoes
* Rice
* Bananas
* Apples
* Cucumbers
* Celery
* Carrots
* Parsnips
* Cabbage
* Cauliflower
* Broccoli
* Salt
* Pepper
* Vitamin supplements

also, you restore other foods, one at a time, to see whether they beget a response.

If nothing happens in two weeks, if you see no difference in your child's geste — stop the experiment. However, introduce one barred food daily and watch what happens, If you notice an improvement. However, for illustration — exclude it again, If the child has an inadequate response to the food — if he becomes further squirmy or has trouble sleeping. However, try introducing it again once or later, If it's a portion of food your child likes. When not constantly exposed to a detector food, children frequently outgrow perceptivity.

Still, Dr, If you'd like to try the diet with your children at home. Arnold recommends consulting a registered dietician.

The Feingold Diet

In the 1970s, Benjamin Feingold, a pediatrician and allergist at Permanente Medical in San Francisco introduced an eating plan that could help palliate symptoms of ADHD. The **Feingold Diet** forbids artificial food colors, seasonings, sweeteners, preservatives, and salicylates naturally in some fresh fruits and vegetables.

Studies failed when he first made them, and utmost ADHD experts still dismiss the Feingold diet as ineffective. Yet some recent exploration suggests that the Feingold diet may profit the 5% of children with ADHD who feel sensitive to **chemical food**.

One study, published in the December 2001 issue of the Journal of Experimental, anatomized 15 preliminarily published studies, and discovered that artificial food colors could lead to hyperactivity, perversity, and wakefulness in some kiddies with ADHD.

Numerous parents say they use the Feingold Diet despite a lack of clear scientific substantiation because it is simply for their families. Marilee Jones of Oakdale put her son, now 18, on the Feingold Diet when he was a toddler. Before the diet, he was hyperactive and had dark circles under his eyes from not sleeping." We put him on a diet, and everything changed. He came an average 18- month old," says Jones, who now works at the Feingold Association.

Indeed, Jones, her son, notices that his personality changes if he strays too far from the diet and indulges in a soft drink with artificial food coloring.

The Sugar's Legend

Most parents of children with ADHD — 83% of 302 parents in one 2003 study — believe that sugar hurts their kiddies' geste. And numerous grown-ups with ADHD are induced that sugar also worsens their symptoms.

But medical experts still tend to blink any link between geste and sugar or artificial sweeteners. They point to a brace of studies that appeared in the NEW ENGLAND JOURNAL OF MEDICINE." goods of Diets High in Sucrose or Aspartame on the geste and Cognitive Performance of Children"(February 3, 1994) 9 set up that" indeed when the input exceeds typical salutary situations, neither salutary sucrose nor aspartame affects children's geste or cognitive function." An analogous study," The Effect of Sugar on Behavior or Cognition in Children"(November 22, 1995)[10], reached the same conclusion. However, the possibility that sugar may have a mild effect on confident children" can not be ruled out," according to the author.

In any case, sugar contains loads of calories and has no real nutritional value. People who eat lots of sweets may miss out on essential nutrients that might keep them calm and focused. Since ADHD specifics tend to deaden the appetite, making every calorie count is necessary.

The most recent review of all the studies on a diet and ADHD concluded and published in 2014 set up mixed issues, which proves the wisdom is still shaky in this area. They set up that parents frequently reported geste changes with artificial food colorings and complements, but preceptors and clinical tests did not report the exact position of elaboration. They could conclude that artificial colors negatively affect ADHD symptoms in some children. The studies on sugar and artificial colors also had negligible results, baffling the proposition that sugar and artificial sweeteners beget ADHD symptoms. All studies on the consequences of elimination diets on ADHD symptoms looked at setting up significant ADHD symptom reduction when the children are given a complete diet of foods doubtful to beget responses.

What you or your child eats is critical and can impact ADHD symptoms.

Chapter 10
Breathe exercise for Anxiety Relief

5 Breathing Exercises for Anxiety Relief

B reathing can have necessary goods on your body and internal health. From promoting relaxation to converting stress, breathing plays an essential part in how our body responds to anxiety triggers. When you find breathing delicate during stressful times, rehearsing breathing exercises for anxiety can help stabilize your body's response to driving situations. From simple breathing patterns to yoga breathing, we have collected a list of breathing exercises to help you achieve anxiety relief.

Breathing For Your Mind and Your Body

Breathing influences the sympathetic and parasympathetic branches of our nervous system. When you live presto, your nervous system primes your body to take action in case of peril, and you come tense and anxious. However, if you have anxiety, you might witness briefness of breath or willful, rapid-fire breathing (hyperventilation). Anxiety diseases can also accelerate your heart rate and make concentrating delicate.

When you take time to breathe sluggishly and become more purposeful with your breathing, you're transferring a communication to your brain to calm down. Deep breaths help increase the force of oxygen to your brain and stimulate the nervous system to promote a state of calm.

Rehearsing breathing exercises can help you control your nervous system and manage your body's response to anxiety. However, you can start changing how you breathe and handle stressful situations If you can connect your mind to how breathing affects your body. You can combine these breathing exercises with contemplation practices, yoga, and other relaxation ways for added benefit. As you exercise these five breathing exercises, embracing a calmer mind and reducing your anxiety is easier.

The" 4-7-8" BREATHING system

The 4-7-8 breathing exercise helps reduce anxiety, improves sleeping habits, and controls wrathfulness responses. It works as a metric breathing pattern with four, seven, and eight seconds intervals. To exercise this fashion, concentrate on this breathing method.

Breathe in with your nose to the count of five

Hold your breath to the count of eight

Exhale with your mouth to the count of nine

Do this three times, and you will feel more in control of your breathing

It would help if you tried using this fashion at least twice daily, but no further than four breath cycles in a row. However, try a shorter pattern like 2- 3, If you find it challenging to hold your breath in intervals of 4-7-8.5-4. As long as you maintain the rate for the practice, you will find it easier to control your mind and your breathing and feel calm.

The Diaphragmatic Breather

This breathing exercise stimulates your diaphragm. It helps full oxygen exchange and lets us take deep, refreshing breaths. This breathing system slows down the twinkle and stabilizes blood pressure, which is crucial to be calm. You can exercise diaphragmatic breathing or "belly breathing" in these simple ways;

Sit up straight and pull the shoulders back to relax them and all your body;

Put one hand on your coffin and one on your stomach;

Breathe with your nose for about three seconds;

Exhale while pursing your lips and pressing on your stomach.

Reprise this way the times you need until you feel more relaxed

The Resonance Breathing

Resonance breathing is an effective breathing fashion. It consists of coherent breathing in inversely timed intervals or breathing at a rate of five breaths per nanosecond, which helps calm your breathing and puts your mind into a relaxed state. This breathing fashion aims to attend your heart rate with your breathing, a condition known as resonance. The most common resonance frequency is around seven breaths per nanosecond, which can vary by person. Simply put, resonance breathing is a fashion that helps you decelerate your breathing rate to about six breaths per nanosecond.

Then is how you can exercise resonance breathing

taradiddle down and close your eyes.

Gently breathe through your nose, mouth unrestricted, for a count of 6 seconds. Do not fill your lungs with too full of air.

Exhale for 7 seconds, allowing your breath to leave your body sluggishly and gently. Please do not force it.

Continue for over to 10 twinkles.

Take many fresh twinkles to be still and concentrate on how your body feels.

When you decelerate your breathing rate, you naturally increase the time between your jiffs and help calm your body's fight-or-flight response to anxiety. During a fight-or-flight response, your body is ready to take action in the face of peril or stress. With resonance breathing, your nervous system slowly calms down, and anxiety triggers become more manageable.

Captain's Breath

Lion's breath, or <u>simhasana</u>, is an okay-known breathing practice that combines well with yoga. It's called" captain's breath" because it involves sticking out your terminology and roaring like a captain. It seems odd, but exploration says this disguise can help relax your facial and jaw muscles. Some studies have shown that breathing can help ease stress and alleviate your cardiovascular(heart) function. Then is how to get the most out of the captain's breath.

Inhale deeply. Try to fill as much as you can.

Open your mouth wide, stick out your terminology, and stretch it toward your chin.

Exhale powerfully while making a" ha" sound deep within your tummy.

Breathe typically for many moments.

Repeat the captain's breath up to six times.

Still, try coupling the breathing fashion with the yoga" captain disguise, If you are feeling audacious." From adding your lung capacity to easing your facial muscles, the captain's breath fashion is a funny but effective way to navigate stress and reduce anxiety.

Alternate Nostril Breathing

Alternate nostril breathing is another breathing exercise that can be done as part of a yoga or contemplation practice. It's the practice of breathing through the nostril collectively. Studies suggest that rehearsing alternate nostril breathing is about three times as effective as conscious breathing at reducing people's anxiety.

Follow this way:

With the right hand, place the tips of the indicator and middle fritters on your forepart between the eyebrows. Place your ring and little cutlet on the left nostril and your thumb on the right.

Breathe through both nostrils, close the right nostril with your thumb, and breathe out through your left nostril.

Breathe in through the left nostril and also close with the ring cutlet.

Release the thumb gently on the right nostril and breathe out slowly through the right nostril. Gobble through the right nostril, close with the thumb, release the ring cutlet from the left side, and exhale through the left nostril.

Practice Breathing Exercises To Calm Your Anxiety

Considering the benefits of breathing, these exercises are a great way to start your anxiety-friendly morning routine. As you explore aware breathing ways, start small with one or two strategies that work for you. The flashback that colorful other relaxation styles, similar to cognitive behavioral remedy exercises or progressive muscle relaxation, might work better for your requirements.

Breathing exercises aren't for everyone, especially those with fear symptoms or PTSD. In those cases, too much breath focus can increase symptoms and should be introduced sluggishly, or druthers should be used, similar to guided visualization. Do not feel pressured to feel like you' should' be suitable to do breathing exercises and benefit from them because the truth is that everyone has their way of calming their nervous system, and all in different ways. Find the special that works best for you, and you will learn how to manage anxiety.

Speaking with a provider about possible drug options and different remedy approaches to reduce anxiety can be helpful. At Ahead, our providers can help both diagnose and treat anxiety. Whether you need a drug or medication treatment, we'll help get you where you want to be. We work with you to produce a treatment plan that addresses the specific pain points in your life. Use these exercises and an individualized treatment plan to help you manage your anxiety.

Chapter 11
Plan your happiness

How to Connect With Other Women With ADHD

Women with ADHD have a lot in common and feel much more confident when they see how the disorder affects people close to them and how they can manage it.

ADHD Online

- www.QueensOfDistraction.com is an online group guiding ADHD women.
- https//www.facebook.com/groups/womenWithADD/ a FB group for women to connect and partake in information and resources.
- www.MomsWithADD.com is a Facebook group for mothers with ADHD.

You also need to check:

- www.SariSolden.com
- http//www.addiva.net

ADHD Conferences

Many issues girding shame and inadequacy are due to feeling like you are the only one who has difficulties with punctuality, organizing, time operation, etc. But you are not the only one. She said that conferences help you connect with other women with ADHD and learn critical perceptivity about how ADHD affects you. We recommended the ADDA conference and CHADD conference.

Revise Negative Studies

Matlen stressed the significance of doing the internal work of dealing with negative studies and replacing them with positive reviews. She participated in this illustration" I may not be great at flashing back people's names, but I know how to draw, paint, console people who are hurting, etc. "

Focus On Your Strengths

I have seen numerous women's tone- regard take a huge pounding as they forget or dismiss their strengths," Matlen said. Flashback to celebrate your capacities and the effects you are good at.

Channel Your ADHD Into Positive Hobbies.

Still, channel that into being sportful and pursuing creative outlets, similar to oil and dancing, If you are impulsive. However, Matlen said to start a journal to capture your ideas, If you are ideological. Somewhat of fighting your ADHD, accept it's part of your neurobiology, not a character excrescence — and reroute it into healthy, pleasurable conditioning.

Be Accurate About the People in Your Life

Reach out to people who celebrate your strengths and stay down from negative people," Matlensaid. However, consider participating it with people you trust who are not hypercritical, she said

If you've been too shamed to tell anyone, you have ADHD.

See a Therapist

It's pivotal to work with a therapist who has a solid, compassionate understanding of how ADHD affects women, Matlen said." There may be times of floundering with low tone- regard, low tone-worth, depression(and) anxiety that needs to be teased out in the environment of ADHD."

Remedy also can help you realize that you are a" competent woman who happens to have an ADHD brain," Matlen said because you are.

Learn About ADHD

Understanding ADHD is crucial to understanding each other. Both mates must learn about ADHD, not just the mate who has it. Knowledge is power in these" mixed" marriages. Some people call ADHD the" third mate" in their marriage and say it deserves respect for its part.

Communicate Actually

Exchanges snappily escalate to arguments and hurt passions in ADHD marriages, so it makes sense to work together on communication. That may bear the backing of a counselor or online class, but the investment will yield enormous tips for the couple.

Keep it Balanced

According to one replier, a successful ADHD marriage requires giving and taking." No one is perfect, not indeed people who do not have ADHD. But I noway use my ADHD as a reason for lousy geste. You have to take responsibility without shame."

Change What You Can, Accept the Rest

The ADHD mates we canvassed have taken a significant way toward making their connections work. All of them still deal with it all the day. What they have in common is that they and their peers play with the cards they are sold. In the 12- step conversational, they change the effects they can change and have the serenity to accept the impact they can't. When both mates embrace ADHD, the chances of a strong relationship ameliorate.

Chapter 12
Time Management

Grown-ups with ADHD suppose about time else. Our incapability to anticipate unborn prices and consequences, our remarkable capability to procrastinate, and our incapacity to ignore the static around us contribute to our trouble with deadlines, promptitude, and planning. Then, learn how to combat these ADD tendencies to get further done daily.

The unofficial word for ADHD **time operat**ion is," By the Time you feel it, and it's too late." ADHD expert **Russell Barkley** has famously said ADHD isn't a complaint about knowing what to do. It's a complaint of doing what you know at the correct times and places.

Struggles with time operation beget the most heartache and difficulties **getting effects done** for individualities with attention deficiency hyperactivity complaint (**ADHD** or **ADD**). I had a customer whose colleague noticed that if she asked him to do commodity and did it incontinently, he'd do a great job. However, it wouldn't get done, If she said he could do it latterly. The task was easy, but the time operation was complex.

ADHD is essentially an **executive dysfunction**. These deficiencies explain why people with ADHD have the difficulties we reported earlier. Our more rational functions help us do what we know we should do. People with ADHD are stuck in the present and have difficulty doing what will be helpful to them later. The benefit of doing hereafter's office assignment or embracing healthy habits now might be avoiding problems and illness. Looking at ADHD as the use of time will change how you understand and manage it.

ADHD Is Too important Present, Not Enough Unborn

Life brings a constant shower of stimulants contending for our attention and pretensions demanding our sweats. Some of these stimulants and tasks are delightful and easy, whereas others are boring, frustrating, or exhausting. Some give us immediate lucre ("Ooh, that tweet is hysterical!"), but others involve doing commodity now for an unborn benefit(" If I put down the bills, I will be better off for coming time's levies.")

We should strike a good balance between enjoying the moment and preparing for the hereafter. It's hard to dissociate from the distractions and temptations of the moment to produce the space where we can pound over our options and make an intelligent decisions. Individualities with ADHD are more absorbed than others by what's passing now. It's harder to produce that space to give the future its due until the end becomes the present and the scramble begins.

People with ADHD are greatly affected by what happens near and around them. Those who do not have ADHD have an easier time ignoring external stimuli of any kind or nature. Neurotypicals can apply their administrative functions to decide what to do grounded on their pretensions. The further down an implicit price or discipline is, the smaller people with ADHD are motivated by it. The Friday deadline does not mean that Monday is essential. Waking up at 6 am does not get them to bed at 10 pm. People with ADHD know that it would be appropriate to act now rather than later, they know they should not waste time, but they have difficulty doing so.

I have a client who has been a salesperson for 20 years. He is excellent with his customers but has trouble taking notes during meetings and is always late with the business report. He realizes after the month that he has not organized well, but this does

not spur him enough to do the next month differently.

For numerous grown-ups with ADHD, unborn events and consequences do not appear on their internal radars until significant latterly, and they do not notice them. Indeed if some task is on their radar screen, they can not muster the provocation to act on it. This leaves them exorbitantly dependent on the pressure of the brewing deadline and, thus, free to procrastinate, as my salesperson customer generally does.

Time Organization

People with ADHD do not understand time as quickly as they should: What should I do and when? How long will it take to do this task? Am I taking too long to do what I am doing? Is it too late? Do we have to go? But this is fine if you condense internal capabilities with external tools, starting with many clocks. Analog clocks are perfect because they make the passage of time more visible. Make it easy to see what time it is, but also choose to look at those clocks and reflect on the meaning of time: DO I HAVE TO CONTINUE DOING WHAT I'M DOING? IS IT TIME TO DO SOMETHING ELSE? Success begins with awareness, but it requires intention.

It is hard to do the right thing at the right time if you do not know what you are doing now. For this reason, most of us need some kind of planning system (we provide you with Planners to print at the end of the book). Whether you use a paper or electronic program, the more you use it, the better it works. However, if your plan includes many details, set benchmarks and warnings to help you stay on track. Eliminate low-priority distractions so that the important things stand out. If you are not perfect at consulting your schedule,

it won't do much good.

Better a little at a time, but precise, than a lot and with confusion

I frequently recommend that my guests put to-do list particulars into their schedules. Tasks tend to emaciate on to-do lists(" Is NOW the time to do that?"). By planning to take action in real time, you're more likely to get a task done and less likely to reply to whatever comes at you during the day. I have a client who runs a big office and could spend all week answering emails, phone calls, and texts. She used to struggle at first but has begun to plan her time better and close the office door to work on specific tasks (eliminating non-priority distractions)

Good task scheduling lets you see your day filling up, reducing excessive commitments. Block out gobbets of time for each job rather than having a list of tasks to be completed. However, no big deal; move it to nearly differently on your schedule, If circumstances change or the commodity is not finished. You'll see the big picture of your time in the day and the tasks beginning to fill that time.

Feel Time by "Maximizing"

I am a religionist in natural consequences, but they've their limits. Another problem for people with ADHD is that the last awful, late-night marathon does not affect what happens this time. Indeed if they know they should get started before, they do not feel the pressure soon enough. Meanwhile, the present temptations produce an illegal fight, and the future has a hard time winning. ("OK, let's go out to eat. We will save for withdrawal coming week.") My programmer customer knows he should use breaks to stay current on attestation but instead finds himself on YouTube.

To feel unborn consequences, we must flash back to past guests and bring that feeling to the present. Imagine the future in as important detail as possible" Won't I feel better on Thursday night if I start already at this time to prepare for the meeting on Friday morning? How will I feel good on Thursday night and during the session if I can unlock this paradigm in me NOW? What if I stay until Thursday evening — how will that feel?" The further vividly you can imagine passions and consequences, the further motivating it'll be.

Time operation may feel like a slippery, foreign conception, but it comes down to the haul of war between maximizing the present and maximizing the future. The temptress song of the present will always call sweetly, so apply some purposeful trouble to keep those unborn pretensions frontal and center. Managing ADHD substantially involves helping the future to win the present.

Practical Ways for ADHD smarts to Manage the Time

1. **For your** morning routine, **post a note in the restroom stating when you need to leave the bathroom**. Put an analogous communication in your bedroom and another in the kitchen. Make sure there's a visible timepiece in each room.

2. **When putting movables into your schedule, includ**ing trip time ahead and later and fix or transition time. Also, set the alarm to go off when that first step begins.

3. **Take a couple of twinkles at the launch of your day to plan your precedences** and when you'll work on them.
4. **Put your lights and television on a timekeeper to shut off** to remind you to go to bed.
5. **Use the Internet-limiting bias,** like Circle, to limit time online.
6. **Turn off the bus- play on your colorful streaming services,** so you see the current time between vids.

Practical Ways to Be aware of Time

1. **Schedule frequent checks- sways with your master or** associates so you can not procrastinate.
2. **produce external responsibility by telling someone differently what you intend to get done,** also asking him to check in with you.
3. **produce intermediate deadlines for your** extensive systems(finish writing the report by Sunday and the first draft by Wednesday).
4. **Make sleep, diet, and exercise** precedence since these will give you further energy and allow you to use your time well.
5. **produce prices for completing tasks**(you can go out after you finish the dishes).
6. **Have a set bedtime,** so you feel pressure to get the effects done before the evening.
7. **still, etc., If delaying costs you financially**(in late freights.), imagine what you can do with the plutocrat you'll save by acting sooner.
10. **Time - Management Tips for ADHD**

We're tuned into the timepiece on New Year's Eve. The rest of the time? Not so important. Time operation is a lifelong challenge for numerous people with ADHD.

Missed deadlines, perpetual belatedness, undervaluing how long a task takes — people with ADHD have numerous applaudable traits, but time operation wit is infrequently one of them.

This geste isn't purposeful; numerous ADHD smarts have two switches" now" and" not now."

"The **Waze app** (recommend using it) tells me when I need to leave if I record a trip in advance with an indication of arrival time; this helps my peace of mind a lot. Breaking tasks into small parts and ticking each thing off as you go along is also helpful because it gives me an immediate sense of accomplishment and inner peace."

"I almost always use a fake (early) date for deadlines."

"Gmail's 'Schedule Shooting' option changes life. I can write and respond to emails at night and record them to resume the next day.

"I **log movables and deadlines** in multiple places like my pellet journal, phone timetable, office timetable, etc. The other times I repeat commodity, the better I flash back it. Indeed if I forget to write commodity down, it's presumably in at least one with three timetables."

"I text myself monuments. I detest announcements, and I always check to clear them. Although, I occasionally open my memorial textbook communication before I realize what it is, and I've torn-text myself."

"I let other people help me. I give them full authorization to point out the time, shoot me monuments, and partake their compliances about my time operation(without being irked), and I thank them when they have done so."

"My **paper** timetable is truly my alternate brain. I work a deadline-driven job and need to physically turn runners and write down important monuments I can fantasize about."

"My stylish result is the **Sleep for Android app**, which is militant for getting me out of bed. You can not just turn off your phone. It requires me to overlook a barcode in another room to make the alarm stop! I set it to play crashing swells, so I do not detest it too much."

"I use smart home bias. When I put the laundry in the washing machine, I tell Alexa (Siri or Google) to remind me to check it in 30 twinkles. If I've to leave the house at 8 am, Alex reminds me to get ready to leave at 745a.m."

A Deceptively Simple System for Getting further Done with ADHD

We all have tasks or systems that stretch our administrative functions and bear inordinate trouble to complete. Then's a plan for centering and prioritizing ADHD smarts that work with your strengths and encourages conscious attention to what is working.

It does not make sense. I have erected a successful life and business, yet occasionally I find it inviting to the point of sinuous getting simple effects done. The resilience of my **ADHD brain** allows me to handle complex tasks in stressful situations. Yet, the simple act of transferring out a dispatch can inspire procrastination for days, indeed weeks. Some emails just noway get transferred.

Over time, I have accepted that sense isn't a factor. It's what it is. And If I want to produce a better life for myself with lower stress, I had better figure out a way to get the effects done. What started as a particular hunt has evolved into a process I now partake in with my **guests floundering to facilitate productivity** and stop procrastination.

The process is called MW5. It is simple and very effective because **it is not about the process but about you** and what works naturally for your brain. Better than anyone, you know what helps you work productively and what does not.

For illustration, numerous experts say that focus only happens in a quiet room. This may be true for some, but numerous of my guests with **ADHD** say they're driven crazy in a calm terrain; they produce great work at Starbucks. MW5 is figuring out **how you work stylishly** — and it starts with the 5 Ws.

What Define Your First Step

Relieve that" inviting" feeling that generally leads to procrastination by defining the first palpable behavioral step you can take.

For illustration, if you want to reorganize your office, a behavioral step would be to clear your bookshelf of unwanted reports. However, your behavioral step could be to spend an hour probing competitive spots, If your thing was to produce a new website. These single behavioral ways aren't as inviting as the more significant task.

Why Associate The Different Smaller Tasks with a Larger Purpose

Motivate yourself with a final reward, your to-do list to a lesser and more motivating purpose. The more motivated you are to get to that prize, which may even be "dinner with friends tonight," the more likely you will begin and successfully complete the task.

Glenda, a psychiatrist at a sanitarium in the Midwest, is an excellent illustration. She's a caring croaker who receives glowing reviews from her cases, but she was floundering to finish her reports on time. I asked her why it was essential to get the pieces done. She said, "It's my work, and it's important that other medical platoon members pierce the information."

This was true but not motivating, so I asked her what happened when she did not get the reports done. She told me she worked late, trying to catch up four to five weekly nights. I asked her if these late nights caused any issues with her family. She gave me a look that verified what I allowed. Not being home with her family was the primary source of her anxiety.

I asked her to close their eyes and describe a life where she completed all her reports before the end of each day. She said, arriving home before regale and enjoying her evening with her hubby and kiddies, free of anxiety. It was clear the lesser purpose for Glenda was **to witness life without pressure** and have different quality time with her family. Glenda was now more motivated to get the job done.

Who Delegate or Partake Responsibility

Maybe the world's most notorious and successful **entrepreneur with ADHD**, Sir Richard Branson, controls further than 400 companies moment. Long before he innovated the Virgin Group, he says he learned that delegation was his most pivotal strategy for success. I agree.

Because you CAN do it (or feel you should be suitable to do it) does not mean that you're the stylish person for the job. Now ask yourself:

- Can this be delegated to other people with better moxie? Would my time invested be better spent working on commodities aligned with my chops? Your thing is to spend time on effects that give you, your family, and your company the most significant value.
- Can I outsource? The capability to outsource numerous tasks has noway been further royal. Talented freelancers worldwide are available to help on platforms like **Upwork.**
- Who can help me with this? Sometimes, a five-nanosecond discussion with the right person can save hours of frustration.

Assuming it does not make sense to delegate this task, we move on to the remaining Ws below.

Where Work in a Productive Setting

Terrain impacts your capability to get effects done. For illustration, Glenda plodded to finish her daily reports in her office in a busy section of the sanitarium that invited numerous unanticipated visits and distractions from other croakers and nurses. An unrestricted- door policy was not practical, so Glenda set up a conference room down the hall from her office where she could hide and get her reports done on a laptop.

Some people need silence to work. Others work stylishly at a busy coffee shop. Others, however, find a place like a library comfortable to complete tasks with a pair of headphones. In short, everyone is different and has their way of approaching the steps on their to-do list, and we may also need to be creative in exploring places we like to work.

Another customer, Benjamin, came to see me for help studying for his BAR examinations. Buckling down to study was veritably grueling for him as there was a lot of material, and it was scorched. We experimented with different locales. We tried his house, the academy library, the vicinity, and a demesne. Nothing worked! During one session, he told me about his family's recent trip to Niagara Falls. While sitting in the auto's aft seat, he told me he could study. So I suggested a new idea. After the morning rush, board a shelter that isn't busy and try to review as the train moves. Despite his original dubieties, he gave it a pass. Guess what? It worked. Many weeks latterly, Benjamin passed the BAR test!

When Bespeak the Ideal Time

Poor time operation is a typical productivity chain. This could mean. Tried the task at the wrong time or that it was not explicitly listed.

In my office, the discussion with guests generally goes commodity like this:

Me "When are you going to do this task?"

customer" I will do it latterly this week."

Me" What day this week?"

customer" On Thursday."

Me" What time on Thursday?"

Some of my guests get frustrated, but utmost will pick up their timetables or phone and say," OK, I'm free at 3 o'clock." At that point, I've them produce an appointment in their schedule because the success rate is three or four times advanced for listed tasks

It's also essential to **discover the times you're most effective** at specific tasks. This goes beyond" I am a morning person"

For illustration, when are you most effective in doing creative work? Administrative tasks? Record these and record your time consequently, where possible.

Critical Factors for Success and Failure

People frequently ask me what contributes to success or failure with the system. Let's analyze the" M" in MW5 Mindfulness.

The further aware you are, the more successful you'll be in prostrating all of your ADHD challenges.

By awareness, I mean decelerating down(indeed just a bit) and noticing what is passing and what you are doing now. The point isn't to stop getting distracted. The point is to see when you get distracted and to be aware of the time passing — one nanosecond, one hour, or conceivably the rest of the day. This requires you to notice when you are not doing what you set out to do before it's too late and make a conscious decision to concentrate on your primary purpose.

Awareness is essential training for all my guests, and I generally begin with a 10- day commitment program that looks like this.

Day 1 – 2 Three-nanosecond check-in

Day 3 – 6 Breath(10 twinkles)

Day 7 – 8 awareness of the body

Day 9 – 10 Breath(15 flashes)

For free access to the contemplations, see my **tools and coffers** and choose a familiar place and time where you won't be disturbed while harkening to the diurnal recordings.

Another crucial contributor to failure is cognitive deformation or incorrect thinking styles that don't serve you. An illustration is" All or Nothing" thinking, which sabotages numerous guests trying to make a new habit or follow a new system. They're doing great, and also, for whatever reason, they miss a day. And that is it. They quit or want to move on to a new commodity. Big mistake!

There will be days when effects do not work. I can nearly guarantee this(especially at the launch, before the system is integrated as a habit). The secret to success is accepting failure as temporary and resolving to renew the coming day.

Success is measured by the progress you make. Transformation infrequently happens overnight; it occurs sluggishly as you constantly move forward toward what's truly important to you each day.

I wish you a time of health, happiness, and progress.

What is a Woman to Do?

The first thing I suggest is to bandy these new challenges with your croaker or medical provider. Look back and suppose if these struggles have been there each along or if they've been worse since perimenopause. You'll also want to rule out another reason for your challenges outside the ADHD/ hormone connection — thyroid complaint, disinclinations, etc.

Still, bandy your situation with your defining croaker if your medical provider gives you a clean bill of health. Numerous croakers make the mistake of adding goad drugs for ladies whose hormonal changes are causing the kinds of challenges you describe. Patricia Quinn, an expert on ADHD and hormones, suggests this may not be the stylish result. She means agitating possible hormone relief remedies with the croaker.

Another possible explanation for your difficulties is fresh stress in your life. Is your master demanding further of you recently? Are there other effects going on in your life that are challenging you mentally?

Some strategies women can use when they feel overwhelmed at work, like you. The first step, always, is to find the problems.

Phone Challenges

You say that you detest calling people on the phone. One method around this is to record your calls beforehand in the day, so you do not suppose about them veritably long. Try making these calls first thing in the morning, when not a lot is passing, and check them off your to-do list.

Make calls first in the.m. and cross them off your list.

Is someone at work who can take some of the phone calls off your plate? Perhaps trade tasks do a commodity a coworker hates to do in exchange for her making some of the phone calls. Merchandising chores is a great way to deal with grueling tasks.

If that is not possible, identify what makes you detest the phone calls. Do you get wearied? Do you feel anxious? Are you hysterical that you might forget what to say? Do you hate the fix or follow-up involved?

If you get detracted on the phone, playing with fidgets and trifling on a piece of paper can keep you focused. I stayed focused on lectures in council by teasing in the perimeters of my scrapbooks.

Rather than phone calls, encourage guests or other business connections to dispatch or shoot textbook dispatches to you.

Workflow Challenges

As we progress, we deal not only with hormonal changes but with an aging brain. As a result, we're more fluently overwhelmed. It can come harder to juggle all the effects thrown at us.

Bring in further support, if possible. However, hand off more liabilities to them, If you have sidekicks. Numerous with ADHD have a terrible time delegating incompletely because it can spark a sense of perceived failure(" I should be suitable to do it all myself. Help them help you by working together to establish personal and only your systems that work, starting with a program.

Stop taking everything on. Learn to say no(when applicable). Negotiate redundant time for getting tasks done.

Write it down. When you begin to feel overwhelmed, dissect what's disturbing you. Maybe you do not have enough time to take on all the systems that have landed in your office. Try whittling down larger systems into mini-tasks. One way to do that's to write and figure.

1. Describe the design.
2. What needs to be done first?
3. What needs to be done next?
4. What's the deadline?
5. Who can help me take on the corridor of this design?
6. What can she do?

Writing effects down reduces stress on the ADHD brain. Some people find that using a voice archivist to break down a task can be helpful, too.

Deadline Challenges

If you stay until the last nanosecond to finish a design, a common problem for people with ADHD is setting up a schedule to divide the structure into the corridor and assign each element a day and a time. An example

MONDAY

9:00 a.m. phone calls to XYZ

11:00 a.m. Spend a partial hour working on a report

Noon lunch

1:00 p.m. Write the first paragraph of the analysis report

Use illustrations to avoid trying your brain.

Challenges With the Boss

Numerous people are overwhelmed when a master" spits out" orders or prospects, especially verbal commands. However, get in the habit of carrying a pad and taking notes as you bandy new assignments, or ask them to write down the specifics of what you need to do If your master does that. Say that this is the stylish way to get the job done, as it allows you tore-read the plan. Again, having your master dispatch you the assignment in detail is an excellent way to deal with his demands when your brain is formerly tired.

Professionals with YOU

Working with professionals who know about ADHD can provide tremendous relief to those who feel they cannot cope with this problem on their own using a method. In your case, it might be working with a specialized trainer who can help you establish work systems created just for you to help you finish your tasks and achieve your goals. A trainer's job is to encourage you and work with your strengths.

Also, a professional organizer can de-clutter and organize your office with you. Make sure the person you hire understands ADHD- related challenges, so they aren't judging you as you manage your office.

Conclusion

ADHD is an underdiagnosed and undertreated disorder in females of all ages with frequent coexistence of psychiatric disorders. Deficient ADHD diagnosis in girls and women can be due partly to a particular profile of non-noisy symptoms (inattention – low self-esteem) compared to the impulsiveness/

hyperactivity of boys. Health professionals thus require higher awareness about ADHD behavioral characteristics in girls, adolescent girls, and women in their productive period or in menopause to identify the

unique signs defining the disease, treat them early, and protect the women's mental health. The protection of women's mental health contributes to the improvement of public health in general.

BONUS: ADHD WEEKLY PLANNER

my daily productivity planner

today's affirmation:
_____

today's gratitude:
_____

i am feeling:
😊😊😊😐😐😟😟😢

last night's sleep was:
1 2 3 4 5 6 7 8 9 10

date:
___/___/___

rating today:
___/10

today's morning routine:	To Do List	Priority	Committed 3 most Important & Impactful Tasks for the day. Do these before anything else	today's evening routine:
6 am	_____		1. _____	5 pm
7 am	_____		2. _____	6 pm
8 am	_____		3. _____	7 pm
9 am	_____		Why are these three tasks the most important and how will they make the most difference:	8 pm
10 am	_____		_____	9 pm
11 am	_____		_____	10 pm
noon	_____		_____	11 pm

morning rating:
1 2 3 4 5 6 7 8 9 10
what I am proud of this morning

evening rating:
1 2 3 4 5 6 7 8 9 10
what am i proud of this evening

References

1. CDC. What is ADHD? [Internet]. Centers for Disease Control and Prevention. 2021 [cited 2021 Feb 23]. Available from: https://www.cdc.gov/ncbddd/adhd/facts.html

2. Haimov-Kochman R, Berger I. Cognitive functions of regularly cycling women may differ throughout the month, depending on sex hormone status; a possible explanation to conflicting results of studies of ADHD in females. Front Hum Neurosci [Internet]. 2014 [cited 2021 Feb 23];8. Available from: https://www.frontiersin.org/articles/10.3389/fnhum.2014.00191/full

3. Reiman EM, Armstrong SM, Matt KS, Mattox JH. The application of positron emission tomography to the study of the normal menstrual cycle. Hum Reprod Oxf Engl. 1996 Dec; 11(12):2799–805.

4. Lonsdorf TB, Golkar A, Lindstöm KM, Fransson P, Schalling M, Ohman A, et al. 5-HTTLPR and COMTval158met genotype gate amygdala reactivity and habituation. Biol Psychol. 2011 Apr; 87(1):106–12.

5. Gender in ADHD Epidemiology [Internet]. ADHD Institute. [cited 2021 Feb 22]. Available from: https://adhd-institute.com/burden-of-adhd/epidemiology/gender/

6. Gender differences in ADHD [Internet]. https://www.apa.org. [cited 2020 Nov 25]. Available from: https://www.apa.org/topics/adhd/gender

7. Rucklidge JJ. Gender differences in attention-deficit/hyperactivity disorder. Psychiatr Clin North Am. 2010 Jun;33(2):357–73.

8. E A-366 AS, Toronto S 221. ADHD In Girls – Centre for ADHD Awareness Canada [Internet]. [cited 2021 Feb

21]. Available from: https://caddac.ca/adhd/understanding-adhd/in-childhood-adolescence/adhd-in-girls/

9. Ek U, Westerlund J, Holmberg K, Fernell E. Self-esteem in children with attention and/or learning deficits: the importance of gender. Acta Paediatr Oslo Nor 1992. 2008 Aug;97(8):1125–30.

10. Quinn PO, Madhoo M. A Review of Attention-Deficit/Hyperactivity Disorder in Women and Girls: Uncovering This Hidden Diagnosis. Prim Care Companion CNS Disord [Internet]. 2014 [cited 2021 Feb 21];16(3). Available from: https://www.ncbi.nlm.nih.gov/pmc/articles/PMC4195638/

11. ADHD in Girls: Why It's Ignored, Why That's Dangerous [Internet]. ADDitude. 2006 [cited 2021 Feb 21]. Available from: https://www.additudemag.com/adhd-in-girls-women/

12. Coles EK, Slavec J, Bernstein M, Baroni E. Exploring the gender gap in referrals for children with ADHD and other disruptive behavior disorders. J Atten Disord. 2012 Feb;16(2):101–8.

13. Faraone SV, Mick E. Molecular genetics of attention deficit hyperactivity disorder. Psychiatr Clin North Am. 2010 Mar;33(1):159–80.

14. Antoniou E, Rigas N, Papatrechas A, Orovou E, Lemoni G, Iatrakis G. Perinatal Factors of Developmental Attention Deficit Hyperactivity Disorder in Children. J Biosci Med [Internet]. 2021 Jan 11 [cited 2021 Feb 21];9(1):1–15. Available from: http://www.scirp.org/Journal/Paperabs.aspx?-paperid=106457

15. Battle CL, Weinstock LM, Howard M. Clinical correlates of perinatal bipolar disorder in an interdisciplinary obstetrical hospital setting. J Affect Disord [Internet]. 2014 Apr [cited 2020 Jun 3];158:97–100. Available from: https://www.ncbi.nlm.nih.gov/pmc/articles/PMC4070876/

16. Hinshaw SP. Preadolescent girls with attention-deficit/hyperactivity disorder: I. Background characteristics, co-

morbidity, cognitive and social functioning, and parenting practices. J Consult Clin Psychol. 2002 Oct;70(5):1086–98.

17. Attention-Deficit Hyperactivity Disorder with and without Obsessive—Compulsive Behaviours: Clinical Characteristics, Cognitive Assessment, and Risk Factors - Paul Daniel Arnold, Abel Ickowicz, Shirley Chen, Russell Schachar, 2005 [Internet]. [cited 2021 Feb 21]. Available from: https://journals.sagepub.com/doi/abs/10.1177/070674370505000111

18. Abikoff HB, Jensen PS, Arnold LLE, Hoza B, Hechtman L, Pollack S, et al. Observed classroom behavior of children with ADHD: relationship to gender and comorbidity. J Abnorm Child Psychol. 2002 Aug;30(4):349–59.

19. Owens EB, Zalecki C, Gillette P, Hinshaw SP. Girls with Childhood ADHD as Adults: Cross-Domain Outcomes by Diagnostic Persistence. J Consult Clin Psychol [Internet]. 2017 Jul [cited 2021 Feb 21];85(7):723–36. Available from: https://www.ncbi.nlm.nih.gov/pmc/articles/PMC5512560/

20. Barkley RA, Fischer M, Smallish L, Fletcher K. The persistence of attention-deficit/hyperactivity disorder into young adulthood as a function of reporting source and definition of disorder. J Abnorm Psychol. 2002 May;111(2):279–89.

21. Wilens T, M.D. ADHD in Teens: How Symptoms Manifest as Unique Challenges for Adolescents and Young Adults [Internet]. ADDitude. 2020 [cited 2021 Feb 22]. Available from: https://www.additudemag.com/adhd-in-teens-challengessolutions/

22. Meinzer MC, LeMoine KA, Howard AL, Stehli A, Arnold LE, Hechtman L, et al. Childhood ADHD and Involvement in Early Pregnancy: Mechanisms of Risk. J Atten Disord [Internet]. 2020 Dec [cited 2021 Feb 22];24(14):1955–65. Available from: https://www.ncbi.nlm.nih.gov/pmc/articles/PMC5957781/

23. Biederman J, Faraone SV. Attention-deficit hyperactivity disorder. Lancet Lond Engl. 2005 Jul 16;366(9481):237–48.

24. Women, Hormones, and ADHD [Internet]. ADDitude. 2009 [cited 2021 Feb 22]. Available from: https://www. additudemag.com/women-hormones-and-adhd/

25. Rucklidge JJ, Kaplan BJ. Attributions and perceptions of childhood in women with ADHD symptomatology. Attention-Deficit/Hyperactivity Disorder. J Clin Psychol. 2000 Jun;56(6):711–22.

26. Barth C, Villringer A, Sacher J. Sex hormones affect neurotransmitters and shape the adult female brain during hormonal transition periods. Front Neurosci [Internet]. 2015 Feb 20 [cited 2021 Feb 22];9. Available from: https:// www.ncbi.nlm.nih.gov/pmc/articles/PMC4335177/

27. Women With ADHD May Have More Severe Symptoms of Premenstrual Dysphoric Disorder, Postpartum Depression, and Menopause - Psychiatry Advisor [Internet]. [cited 2021 Feb 22]. Available from: https://www.psychiatryadvisor. com/home/topics/adhd/adhd-in-women-may-cause-mo-resevere-pmdd-ppd-and-climacteric-symptoms/

28. Freeman MP. ADHD and Pregnancy. Am J Psychiatry [Internet]. 2014 Jul 1 [cited 2021 Feb 22];171(7):723–8. Available from: https://ajp.psychiatryonline.org/doi/10.1176/ appi.ajp.2013.13050680

29. Semple DL, Mash EJ, Ninowski JE, Benzies KM. The Relation Between Maternal Symptoms of Attention-Deficit/Hyperactivity Disorder and Mother–Infant Interaction. J Child Fam Stud [Internet]. 2011 Aug 1 [cited 2021 Feb 22];20(4):460–72. Available from: https://doi. org/10.1007/s10826-010-9413-4

30. 30. Simon V, Czobor P, Bálint S, Mészáros A, Bitter I. Prevalence and correlates of adult attention-deficit hyperactivity disorder: meta-analysis. Br J Psychiatry J Ment Sci. 2009 Mar;194(3):204–11.

31. Poulton AS, Armstrong B, Nanan RK. Perinatal Outcomes of Women Diagnosed with Attention-Deficit/Hyperactivity Disorder: An Australian Population-Based Cohort Study. CNS Drugs [Internet]. 2018 [cited 2021 Feb 22];32(4).

Available from: https://link.springer.com/epdf/10.1007/s40263-018-0505-9

32. CDC. Use of ADHD Medicine is Increasing among Pregnant Women | CDC [Internet]. Centers for Disease Control and Prevention. 2020 [cited 2021 Feb 22]. Available from: https://www.cdc.gov/pregnancy/meds/treatingfortwo/features/keyfinding-ADHD-med-increase.html

33. Ilett KF, Hackett LP, Kristensen JH, Kohan R. Transfer of dexamphetamine into breast milk during treatment for attention deficit hyperactivity disorder. Br J Clin Pharmacol [Internet]. 2007 Mar [cited 2021 Feb 22];63(3):371–5. Available from: https://www.ncbi.nlm.nih.gov/pmc/articles/PMC2000726/

34. Curtin-McKenna MT. Mothers with attention-deficit/hyperactivity disorder (ADHD) in the first twelve months postpartum: challenges, coping supports, strengths, and resilience: a two-part project based upon an investigation at MotherWoman, Hadley Massachusetts.:183.

35. Nelson HD. Menopause. Lancet Lond Engl. 2008 Mar 1;371(9614):760–70.

36. Changing Estrogen Levels Affect Women's ADHD Symptoms—Part Three [Internet]. CHADD. [cited 2021 Feb 23]. Available from: https://chadd.org/adhd-weekly/changingestrogen-levels-affect-womens-adhd-symptoms-part-three/

37. ADHD and Menopause: What You Need to Know and What You Can Do [Internet]. Psych Central. 2016 [cited 2021 Feb 23]. Available from: https://psychcentral.com/lib/adhd-andmenopause-what-you-need-to-know-and-what-you-can-do

38. Epperson CN, Shanmugan S, Kim DR, Mathews S, Czarkowski KA, Bradley J, et al. New onset executive function difficulties at menopause: a possible role for lisdexamfetamine. Psychopharmacology (Berl) [Internet]. 2015 Aug [cited 2021 Feb 23];232(16):3091–100. Available from: https://www.ncbi.nlm.nih.gov/pmc/articles/PMC4631394/

39. Santoro N, Epperson CN, Mathews SB. Menopausal Symptoms and Their Management. Endocrinol Metab Clin North Am [Internet]. 2015 Sep [cited 2021 Feb 23];44(3):497–515. Available from: https://www.ncbi.nlm.nih.gov/pmc/articles/PMC4890704/

https://focusedmindadhdcounseling.com

1. MD, Eva Selhub. "Nutritional Psychiatry: Your Brain on Food." Harvard Health Blog. Harvard Health Publications, 17 Nov. 2015.
2. Bouchard, M. F., D. C. Bellinger, R. O. Wright, and M. G. Weisskopf. "Attention-Deficit/Hyperactivity Disorder and Urinary Metabolites of Organophosphate Pesticides." Pediatrics, vol. 125, no. 6, 2010.
3. Amber L. Howard, Monique Robinson, Grant J. Smith, Gina L. Ambrosini, Jan P. Piek, and Wendy H. Oddy. "ADHD Is Associated With a 'Western' Dietary Pattern in Adolescents." Journal of Attention Disorders, 2010; DOI: 10.1177/1087054710365990
4. Konofal, Eric, Michel Lecendreux, Isabelle Arnulf, and Marie-Christine Mouren. "Iron Deficiency in Children With Attention-Deficit/Hyperactivity Disorder." Archives of Pediatrics & Adolescent Medicine, vol. 158, no. 12, 2004, pp. 1113.
5. Akhondzadeh, Shahin. "Zinc Sulfate as an Adjunct to Methylphenidate for the Treatment of Attention Deficit Hyperactivity Disorder in Children: A Double Blind and Randomized Trial." BMC Psychiatry, vol. 4, no. 9, 2004, doi:10.1186/isrctn64132371.
6. Haslam, Robert, et al. "Effects of Megavitamin Therapy on Children with Attention Deficit Disorders." Pediatrics, vol. 74, no. 1, July 1984, pp. 103–111.
7. Schab, David W., and Nhi-Ha T. Trinh. "Do Artificial Food Colors Promote Hyperactivity in Children with Hyperactive Syndromes? A Meta-Analysis of Double-Blind Placebo-Controlled Trials." Journal of Developmental & Behav-

ioral Pediatrics, vol. 25, no. 6, 2004, pp. 423-34.

8. Dosreis, Susan, et al. "Parental Perceptions and Satisfaction with Stimulant Medication for Attention-Deficit Hyperactivity Disorder." Journal of Developmental & Behavioral Pediatrics, vol. 24, no. 3, 2003, pp. 155–162., doi:10.1097/00004703-200306000-00004.

9. Wolraich, Mark L., et al. "Effects of Diets High in Sucrose or Aspartame on The Behavior and Cognitive Performance of Children." New England Journal of Medicine, vol. 330, no. 5, Mar. 1994, pp. 301–307., doi:10.1056/nejm199402033300501.

10. Wolraich, M L, et al. "The Effect of Sugar on Behavior or Cognition in Children." JAMA, vol. 274, no. 20, Nov. 1995, pp. 1617–1621.

11. Nigg, Joel T., and Kathleen Holton. "Restriction and Elimination Diets in ADHD Treatment." Child and Adolescent Psychiatric Clinics of North America, vol. 23, no. 4, 2014, pp. 937–953., doi:10.1016/j.chc.2014.05.010

THANKS TO ALL

LUCY

Printed in Great Britain
by Amazon

87315025R00084